CONTENTS

POCKET GUIDES

TO THE PRIMARY CURRICULUM

Number

Richard English

Provides the knowledge you need
to teach the primary curriculum

Author
Richard English

Editor
Kate Pearce

Assistant Editor
David Sandford

Cover design
Joy White
Rachel Warner

Designer
Rachael Hammond

Illustrations
Gary Davies

Cover photograph
Calvin Hewitt

Published by Scholastic Ltd,
Villiers House,
Clarendon Avenue,
Leamington Spa,
Warwickshire CV32 5PR

Text © 2000 Richard English
© 2000 Scholastic Ltd

1 2 3 4 5 6 7 8 9 0   0 1 2 3 4 5 6 7 8 9

British Library Cataloguing-in-
Publication Data
A catalogue record for this book is
available from the British Library.

ISBN 0-590-53895-0

Number

Introduction

T here is a very strong possibility that you are one of the vast majority of primary teachers or trainee-teachers who do not consider themselves to be a mathematics specialist. In the past, a primary teacher was expected to be a 'Jack-of-all-trades' and so inevitably ended up not having to specialize in a particular subject. But few people saw this as a problem, indeed it was always seen as one of the great strengths of primary education. Most headteachers were more than happy to have a good quality generalist in their team in preference to a specialist with only a narrow range of curriculum expertise. However, things have changed in the last few years so that now the expectations placed on primary teachers are so high that you really do need to be a specialist in all subjects, particularly mathematics, English, Science and ICT.

In mathematics the implementation of the National Numeracy Strategy has meant that many schools and teachers have had to critically evaluate their current practice and make changes to the way they teach the subject. It is no longer acceptable to simply co-ordinate or manage a class of pupils as they work individually through a commercially produced mathematics scheme. In the past the scheme did the job for you but now it is you who is the key factor in the learning process, not the publisher of the

scheme. This is reflected in the high proportion of direct, interactive, whole-class teaching which now typifies the daily mathematics lesson. However, in order to do this effectively you need to have both a high level of subject knowledge *and* the confidence to translate this into stimulating activities for your pupils.

The emphasis and importance of subject knowledge is also reflected in the current requirements for all courses of initial teacher training in England and Wales which are set out in DfEE Circular 4/98. One of the several annexes in the circular describes an initial teacher training curriculum for primary mathematics in which an essential core of knowledge, skills and understanding for all newly qualified teachers is specified. This training curriculum is divided into three parts. The first considers the pedagogical knowledge and understanding required by trainees to secure pupils' progress in mathematics, the second focuses on effective methods of teaching and assessment, and the third identifies a detailed list of mathematical subject knowledge and understanding which all newly qualified teachers must possess.

One of the main aims of this book is to help teachers and trainee-teachers to develop their mathematical subject knowledge and understanding as specified by DfEE Circular 4/98. As the title of the book suggests, the focus is on number, but this has been interpreted to include algebra and so corresponds to the content of the second attainment target of the Mathematics National Curriculum. The table on pages 121–122 provides details of the coverage of this book in relation to the requirements of Circular 4/98.

However, subject knowledge on its own does not make an effective teacher and so this book provides much more than simply a body of facts and procedures for you to learn. An interest and enthusiasm for mathematics are just as important as subject knowledge and so the second main aim of this book is to present mathematics as a subject which is interesting, exciting and therefore capable of motivating and capturing the imagination of pupils. The book therefore contains sections which consider unusual pieces of historical background, amazing facts, common fallacies, important language issues, teaching tips and useful resources. All of these things should help both you and your pupils to enjoy mathematics rather than fear it in the way that you possibly did when you were at school yourself.

A number of sub-headings have been used throughout the book.

Subject facts

Key mathematical subject knowledge is presented and explained in this section using carefully selected worked examples. Here you will find the key facts, definitions, rules, principles and procedures which underpin the teaching of mathematics in the primary school.

Why you need to know these facts

Nobody should learn mathematics just for the sake of it and this basic principle applies to you as well as to the pupils you teach. This section therefore provides a justification for including the chosen material in the preceding section.

Common misconceptions

Mathematics offers everyone the opportunity to 'get hold of the wrong end of the stick' at some stage and so this section tries to identify some of the common errors that pupils and adults often make and the misconceptions they have.

Vocabulary

Mathematics is a rich source of esoteric language which needs to be explained and understood if it is to be used correctly. This section discusses key issues in relation to the use and misuse of mathematical language.

Amazing facts

Here you will find interesting snippets of historical background which provide an insight into why mathematics has evolved into its present form as well as a wide range of truly amazing facts, tips, tricks and activities for you to try with your pupils.

Teaching ideas

This book is not intended to be a resource bank full of teaching activities but in this section you will find general guidelines about teaching a particular aspect of mathematics as well as one or two specific suggestions which you can try out in the classroom.

Resources

It is essential that mathematics is presented as a practical and visually stimulating subject and so provided at the end of each chapter is a section to point you in the direction of a wide range of appropriate resources to support your teaching.

Chapter 1
The structure and language of number

There is no shortage of jargon when it comes to identifying different types of numbers and so you could be forgiven for not knowing your rationals from your irrationals or for thinking that an index is simply the place to look if you want to find a particular page in a book. The aim of this section is to remove the mystery that surrounds some of the language associated with our number system, and to discuss its relevance to teaching and learning in the primary school.

Types of numbers

Natural numbers

Subject facts

These are the numbers which children encounter from an early age when counting objects and so they are often referred to as *counting numbers*. Mathematical dictionaries do not seem to be able to agree on whether zero is a natural number or not but since children are introduced to zero as the number name for 'none' or 'nothing', it seems sensible to include it.

Whole numbers

You might be tempted into thinking that whole numbers are synonymous with natural numbers. However, this would be incorrect. Yes, all of the natural numbers, including zero, are whole numbers but whole numbers can also be negative, that is, less than zero. Whole numbers are also referred to as *integers*.

Cardinal and ordinal numbers

If pupils are using numbers to count objects then they are using *cardinal numbers*, that is, the numbers denote a quantity. For example, a child will associate the number '5' with five objects and so the number refers to the whole set. On other occasions *ordinal numbers* are used to denote position or order and here the number refers to just a single object. For example, the number '5' could refer to the fifth item in a line or page 5 in a book.

Non-integral numbers

If a number is not an integer then it must be a *fraction* or a *decimal*. We tend to use the words 'fraction' and 'decimal' but these are shortened versions of the more precise expressions 'vulgar fraction' and 'decimal fraction', although the former is rather outdated now (and incidentally, should be interpreted as 'common' rather than 'rude' or 'coarse'). The language of fractions and decimals is considered in greater detail in Chapter 3.

A number written in one of these forms can be converted into the other as shown by the examples below:

Fraction	Decimal fraction
$^3/_4$	0.75
$^1/_3$	0.333333333333
$^1/_7$	0.142857142857
$^5/_{11}$	0.454545454545

The first example illustrates how a fraction can have an exact decimal equivalent. The others provide examples of fractions whose decimal equivalents are recurring – that is, the digits follow a repeating pattern that continues forever. The usual way of denoting a recurring decimal is to place a dot above the recurring digit, or above the first and last digit of a recurring sequence, as shown opposite.

$1/3$	=	0.333333333333	=	$0.\dot{3}.$
$1/7$	=	0.142857142857	=	$0.\dot{1}42857\dot{7}$
$5/11$	=	0.454545454545	=	$0.\dot{4}\dot{5}$

Rational and irrational numbers

A *rational number* can be expressed as a fraction, that is in the form a/b, where a and b are integers. Here are a few examples of rational numbers together with their fraction equivalent:

4	$4/1$
1.5	$3/2$
–2.8	$-14/5$
0.003	$3/1000$

It follows then, that an *irrational number* cannot be expressed as a fraction. When written as a decimal fraction these numbers have an infinite number of decimal places and the digits do not recur. When written in this form they must inevitably be rounded to a certain number of decimal places, as illustrated by the examples below.

A common example of an irrational number is the square root of 2, that is, the number which when multiplied by itself gives the answer 2. This is written as $\sqrt{2}$ which is, to eight decimal places, 1.41421356. Even when worked out accurately to hundreds of decimal places there is no pattern in the digits.

Another common example is *pi*, denoted by the symbol π, and used when calculating the circumferences and areas of circles. The value of π to eight decimal places is 3.14159265 but again there is no pattern in the digits even when worked out to hundreds of decimal places.

Real and imaginary numbers

All of the numbers described above are *real numbers* – that is, they actually exist and can be marked on a number line. However, there are some numbers which do not exist in real terms and so cannot be shown on a number line.

These numbers arise when you try to find the square root of any negative number. Try it for yourself by entering –9 on a calculator and then pressing the square root key (√). You should get an error message of some sort. Now let's see if we can find out why the square root of –9 does not exist as a real number. We're trying to find a number which, when multiplied by itself, gives –9. If you try 3, you get 9 and if you try –3 you also get 9 (check with a calculator if you don't believe it). The number we are striving to find does not exist and so we say that it is an *imaginary number*.

The sets of numbers discussed above can be represented on the following Venn diagram:

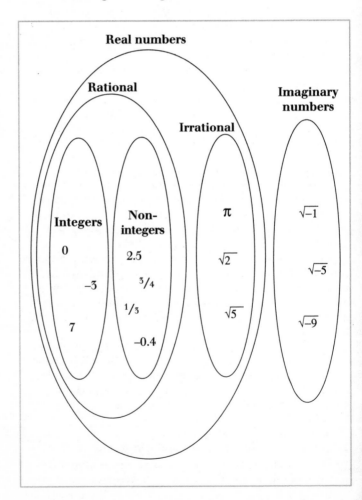

Much of what has been discussed above does not need to be taught to primary pupils in a direct way, although there are some concepts and aspects of the language that will need to be introduced at an appropriate age. Here are a few examples:

● As soon as they start to use simple fractions pupils will need to be familiar with the concept of *whole numbers* and, as their mathematical vocabulary expands during KS2, be introduced to the word *integer* as a more technical expression.

● At the beginning of KS2, pupils should start to encounter negative numbers in everyday contexts such as temperatures or distances above and below sea level.

● Pupils should be introduced to the concept of recurring decimals and the associated notation at the end of KS2 when converting fractions to decimals or when using a calculator for division.

It is also important for you to know these facts in order to strengthen your own subject knowledge so that you can:

● Understand mathematical terminology that you may come across in mathematics textbooks or journals.

● Respond to challenging questions posed by able pupils or colleagues in school. For example, a pupil might ask why they get an error message when they try to work out the square root of a negative number, or a colleague might ask you to explain what an irrational number is.

There are several words which are used to describe the number '0'. *Zero, nought, nothing* and *nil* are four perfectly acceptable words for pupils of all ages to use because they all feature strongly in everyday language. The practice of using the letter sound for 'O', as in 'James Bond 007' or when reciting telephone numbers, is not strictly correct and so should be avoided, although this is not likely to reduce its persistent use.

When dealing with negative numbers such as –3, strictly speaking they should be read as 'negative three' rather than 'minus three'. The term *minus* should only be used in the context of subtraction, not to denote that a number is less than zero. Unfortunately in everyday usage most people say 'minus three'. It is unlikely you have ever heard a weatherperson say 'The temperature tonight will drop to negative three degrees'. Realistically, all you can do is use the correct terminology yourself, encourage pupils to use it, and point out to them that many people get it wrong.

The structure and language of number

Our system of number notation is based on the principle of place value, which enables any number to be represented using only ten digits, 0 to 9. The number systems used by ancient civilizations such as the Chinese, the Greeks, the Egyptians and the Romans, did not use place value and so were often cumbersome and had limitations in terms of the numbers that could be represented.

About 2000 years ago, the Chinese used a horizontal stick notation which developed from the use of the abacus. For example, the number 2 was represented as = , the number 3 as ≡, and these could be combined to represent 23 as = ≡. However, because there was no symbol for zero it was not possible to distinguish 23 from 203, 2003 or 230, although some time later the Chinese did adopt the use of a dot and then a circle to represent zero.

The Romans used different letters to represent the units, the tens, the hundreds and so on. I was used to represent the units, X to represent tens, C to represent hundreds and M to represent thousands. The letters were repeated to denote quantity and so, for example, 23 was represented as XXIII – that is, two tens and three units. Similarly, 423 was represented as CCCCXXIII. (The use of V to denote 5, L to denote 50 and D to denote 500 were relatively late developments in the Roman numeral system.) This notation is still widely understood today but it does have its drawbacks. Firstly, because you need to use a different letter for each power of ten, the size of number that can be represented soon becomes awkward. Secondly, the system does not lend itself to easy methods of pencil and paper arithmetic. Overall, Roman numerals are adequate for representing numbers but not for working with them, for example try working this out quickly:

$$IX + XXI + XI + XI$$

Our present system, which is based on place value and the use of zero, was developed by the Hindus, whose word for zero is *sunya*, meaning 'empty'.

You may remember being told at school that the value of *pi* is $^{22}/_7$ or $3^1/_7$. So, if *pi* is $^{22}/_7$ then surely it must be a rational rather than an irrational number? This much-used fraction is in fact only an approximate value for *pi*. To eight decimal places the fraction is 3.14285714 which is slightly more than the true value of *pi* (3.14159265).

● When introducing pupils to negative numbers, use a vertical number line rather than a horizontal one. This could be displayed on the wall as the scale on a giant thermometer. This vertical scale will allow pupils to quickly get to grips with the language of negative numbers, for example 'rise', 'fall', 'drop', 'below', 'above'. It can also be used to demonstrate other contexts such as distances above and below sea level, or the floors above and below ground level in a building.

● Ask pupils at the upper end of KS2 to investigate the recurring patterns produced when certain fractions are converted to decimals using a calculator. For example they could convert $^1/_9$, $^2/_9$ and $^3/_9$ into decimals and use the pattern to predict what $^4/_9$, $^5/_9$ and so on will be. Elevenths could be investigated in a similar way.

Teaching ideas

Rounding number

Rounding to the nearest 10, 100, and so on

Subject facts

Mathematics is usually thought of as a precise subject but sometimes we don't need to be precise; a rough figure will do. In some cases it is either inappropriate or simply impossible to be exact, for example when giving the distance from the Earth to the Moon or the population of a country. So instead we give an approximate figure which has been rounded appropriately, perhaps to the nearest ten, hundred or thousand.

When rounding to the nearest ten you must decide which ten your number is nearer to. For example when rounding 63 to the nearest ten, the choice is between 60 and 70, and the answer is, of course, 60.

Similarly, when rounding to the nearest hundred you must decide which hundred your number is nearer to, and so in the case of 479 you must choose between 400 and 500, and hopefully opt for the latter.

The much-quoted rule is that you simply look at the digit to the right of the one you are rounding to (for example, look at the tens if you are rounding to the nearest hundred) and if it's 4 or less you round down and if it's 5 or more you round up. But why bother with rules when all you need is a bit of common sense – in other words simply decide which of the two options is nearer.

Golden rules

If the number you are rounding lies exactly halfway between the two options, then by convention you round up. For example 25 to the nearest ten is 30.

Rounding to the nearest whole number

If you need to give a decimal number rounded to the nearest whole number then you can still use the rule described above. You want to round to the nearest unit so you look at the tenths digit and round up or down appropriately. Alternatively, adopt the common sense approach and simply decide which whole number is the nearer.

Rounding to decimal places

If you are happy with the rule then just keep using it! So if you want to give an answer correct to one decimal place (to the nearest tenth) then look at the hundredths and decide whether to round up or down. Similarly, if you want to round to two decimal places (to the nearest hundredth) then look at the thousandths.

Rounding to significant figures

If 5278 is rounded to the nearest thousand to give 5000 then we say that this approximation has one *significant figure* (the 5). Similarly, 28652 rounded to the nearest thousand to give 29000 has two significant figures.

Generally speaking, the number of non-zero digits indicates how many significant figures there are in the approximation. However, sometimes a zero is one of the significant figures. For example, if we round 70487 to the nearest thousand, the answer is 70000 (ie the choice is 70000 or 71000). This has two significant figures, not one, because the 7 and the first zero are both significant. The thousands column has been rounded but it just happened to round to give a zero. Similarly 19615 to the nearest thousand is 20000 (ie the choice is 19000 or 20000) but again this has two significant figures, the 2 and the first zero.

Here are a few more examples to illustrate significant figures:

number	to 1 sig. fig.	to 2 sig. fig.	to 3 sig. fig.
16489	20000	16000	16500
13.87	10	14	13.9
296835	300000	300000 *(1st zero is significant)*	297000
7.941	8	8.0 *(must include the significant zero)*	7.94

Now, just to complicate matters, there's the issue of writing very small decimal numbers (for example, 0.00746) using significant figures. The important point to remember is that the zeros at the start of a number are not significant. The first significant figure in 0.00746 is the 7 and so if you wanted to round this number to one significant figure you must choose between 0.007 and 0.008 and, hopefully, opt for the former.

Here are a few further examples to illustrate significant figures:

number	to 1 sig. fig.	to 2 sig. fig.	to 3 sig. fig.
0.06185	0.06	0.062	0.0619
0.001963	0.002	0.0020 *(final zero is significant and so must be included)*	0.00196
3.0082	3	3.0 *(must include the significant zero)*	3.01

Formal notation

There is a mathematical symbol which means 'is approximately equal to' and its use in the context of rounding is demonstrated below:

$$4.873 \approx 4.9$$

The structure and language of number

Pupils in the primary school are expected to be able to round whole numbers and decimals in various ways.

● Towards the end of KS1, in the context of measurement pupils should be introduced to the idea of giving readings to the nearest unit.

● At the lower end of KS2 pupils should be able to round whole numbers to the nearest 10 or 100.

● Additionally, pupils at the upper end of KS2 should be able to round whole numbers to the nearest 1000, 10000, 100000 and so on, and also be able to round decimals to the nearest whole number, to the nearest tenth and, in the context of money, to the nearest penny (hundredth of a pound).

● Pupils at the upper end of KS2 should be familiar with the symbol ≈.

Pupils at this stage do not need to know about rounding to significant figures, but it is important for you to understand this important concept. You may come across significant figures when reading text books, perhaps relating to other subjects such as science.

Vocabulary

During KS2 pupils should be introduced to appropriate terminology such as *rounding, approximately, approximation* and so on, but it is important to lay a firm foundation for this during KS1 by encouraging pupils to understand and use a variety of everyday language associated with the process of rounding. Expressions such as *about, near to, close to, roughly, just under, just over, more than, less than* and *between* can be introduced to children at a very early age both in the context of number work and shape and space.

Common misconceptions

It is not uncommon for people to round a number to a required level of accuracy in several stages which can lead to errors as illustrated by the example below:

Write 5473 to the nearest thousand.
Round 5473 to the nearest ten to give 5470
Round 5470 to the nearest hundred to give 5500
Round 5500 to the nearest thousand to give 6000

So by rounding an already rounded number, which in turn was a rounded number itself, you produce a final answer of 6000. However, the original number, 5473, is clearly nearer to 5000 than 6000 and so the correct answer is in fact 5000. There are no errors in the individual roundings made at each stage; it is the overall approach which is flawed because this leads you, in the final stage, to be rounding 5500 rather than the original number 5473. To avoid making errors such as this always ensure that you are rounding the original number, not an approximation of that number.

Teaching ideas

Always present the idea of rounding in a visual way by using a large number line displayed on the wall and work through these important stages:
● Identify where the number is on the number line and mark it in some way.
● Remind pupils what it is you are rounding to, for example the nearest 100, the nearest 10, the nearest whole number and so on. Use the expression 'to the nearest...' because this reinforces what rounding is all about.
● If, for example, you are rounding to the nearest ten, ask the children to count on in tens starting at zero. Point to the corresponding numbers on the number line as the pupils call them out. Keep going until you go beyond the number you are rounding.
● Ask pupils to tell you which two numbers of those they have just called out are nearest to the number you are rounding. Mark these on the number line. They should lie either side of the number you are rounding.
● Finally, ask pupils which of the two options is nearer to the number you are rounding. This can be considered in a purely visual way on the number line, or you could reinforce the numerical principles by asking pupils to tell you the number which lies exactly halfway between the two options. Then they must decide whether the number you are rounding is before the halfway point or beyond it.

The process described above might sound a bit long-winded, but it does encourage pupils to think about the ordering and sequencing of numbers and it is based on an understanding of the number system rather than presenting pupils with rules to be learned.

Football match attendance figures are a good resource for rounding practice. These are given exactly and so could be rounded to the nearest thousand, hundred or ten. Sporting performance data, for example times for the 100 metres sprint, which are given to hundredths of a second, could be used to practise rounding to the nearest whole number.

Indices and standard form

Powers or indices

You are probably already familiar with the idea of squaring and cubing a number, for example '7 squared' means 7×7 and can be written as 7^2. Similarly '7 cubed' means $7 \times 7 \times 7$ and can be written as 7^3. These and further examples are shown below:

7^2	$=$	7×7	$=$	49
7^3	$=$	$7 \times 7 \times 7$	$=$	343
7^4	$=$	$7 \times 7 \times 7 \times 7$	$=$	2401
7^5	$=$	$7 \times 7 \times 7 \times 7 \times 7$	$=$	16807

The small number to the right and above the 7 is called the *power* or the *index* (plural *indices*) and so we say, for example, '7 to the power 3' and '7 to the power 4' for 7^3 and 7^4 respectively.

The pattern in the examples shown above can be continued backwards to decide on the meaning and value of '7 to the power 1'. The additional line which can be inserted at the top is clearly:

$$7^1 = 7 = 7$$

Negative indices

You might come across a negative power or index, for example 5^{-2}. This is equal to the *reciprocal* of 5^2. (Note: The reciprocal of a number is the number divided into 1, for example the reciprocal of 3 is $^1/_3$ and the reciprocal of 10 is $^1/_{10}$).

Therefore:

$$5^{-2} = \frac{1}{5 \times 5} = \frac{1}{25} = 0.04$$

and similarly:

$$2^{-3} = \frac{1}{2 \times 2 \times 2} = \frac{1}{8} = 0.125$$

Powers of ten

The positive powers of ten produce the familiar place value column headings as shown below:

10^1	=	10	=	10
10^2	=	10×10	=	100
10^3	=	$10 \times 10 \times 10$	=	1000
10^4	=	$10 \times 10 \times 10 \times 10$	=	10 000
10^5	=	$10 \times 10 \times 10 \times 10 \times 10$	=	100 000

Similarly, the negative powers of ten produce the column headings for the digits to the right of the decimal point:

$$10^{-1} = \frac{1}{10} = \frac{1}{10} = 0.1$$

$$10^{-2} = \frac{1}{10 \times 10} = \frac{1}{100} = 0.01$$

$$10^{-3} = \frac{1}{10 \times 10 \times 10} = \frac{1}{1000} = 0.001$$

$$10^{-4} = \frac{1}{10 \times 10 \times 10 \times 10} = \frac{1}{10000} = 0.0001$$

Standard form

Any number can be written in standard form, although it is more commonly used to denote very large or very small numbers, for example the distance from the Earth to the Sun (93 million miles) or the diameter of a soil amoeba (0.000015 metres). These two distances are shown below in standard form:

$$9.3 \times 10^7$$
$$1.5 \times 10^{-5}$$

The first part is always a number greater than or equal to 1 but also less than 10. The second part is a power of ten. So a number written in standard form comprises a number between 1 and 10 multiplied by a power of ten.

A number written in standard form can be quickly converted to normal notation by simply carrying out the multiplication, for example:

$$9.3 \times 10^7 = 9.3 \times 10\,000\,000 = 93\,000\,000$$

$$1.5 \times 10^{-5} \quad = \quad 1.5 \times 0.00001 \quad = \quad 0.000015$$

When the power of ten is negative, as in the second example above, it is perhaps easier to think of the multiplication by 10^{-5} in terms of division. Multiplying by 0.00001 is the same as dividing by 100000 and so the second example can be worked out like this:

$$1.5 \times 10^{-5} \quad = \quad 1.5 \div 100000 \quad = \quad 0.000015$$

Why you need to know these facts

Much of what has been described above does not need to be taught to primary pupils, although there are one or two aspects which are of direct relevance at the upper end of KS2.

● Pupils should start to recognise 7^2 as '7 squared' and understand what this means.

● Some pupils could be introduced to the idea of writing 100, 1000, 10000 and so on as powers of ten.

● In the context of measurement, pupils will encounter notation such as cm^2 and possibly cm^3, so they will need to know what the abbreviations mean and why they are appropriate.

It is also important for you to know about indices and standard form because these are key mathematical concepts which may crop up in the following situations:

● Standard form notation is commonly used in encyclopaedias and other reference books, particularly when considering scientific data.

● When using a scientific calculator, a very large or very small answer is often displayed in standard form as shown below:

The two parts of the display correspond to the two parts of a number written in standard form. The number displayed above is in fact:

$$4.8735 \times 10^{12} \quad = \quad 4\,873\,500\,000\,000$$

If, when using a spreadsheet, there is not enough room for a very large or very small number to be displayed fully, it may be displayed in standard form as shown below:

	A	B
1	Number	Squared
2	5	25
3	12	144
4	20	400
5	347391	1.207E + 11
6		

The number in cell B5 is in fact:

$$1.207 \times 10^{11} \quad = \quad 120\,700\,000\,000$$

Everyone agrees that a million is $1\,000\,000$ or 10^6 but there is often some confusion over exactly what is meant by a billion. In the past, particularly in Europe, it was often defined as a million million ($1\,000\,000\,000\,000$ or 10^{12}) but now we tend to adopt the American definition and so commonly accept it as being a thousand million ($1\,000\,000\,000$ or 10^9).

Vocabulary

What about the names of other big numbers? Is there really such a thing as a trillion and a zillion? In America a trillion is $1\,000\,000\,000\,000$ or 10^{12} (the same as a European billion), a quadrillion is 10^{15}, a quintillion is 10^{18}, a sextillion is 10^{21}, a septillion is 10^{24}, an octillion is 10^{27}, a nonillion is 10^{30}, and a decillion is 10^{33}. There is no formal definition of what a zillion is and so perhaps we ought to simply think of it as being a very large number!

This leads on to the important issue of what is the biggest number. Pupils are familiar with the fact that Z is the last letter when they recite the alphabet, but what is the last number when they count? It is not possible to identify a specific number as being 'the last' or 'the biggest', the key point being that no matter which number you have, you can always count on further. This unattainable last or biggest number is referred to as infinity and denoted by the symbol ∞.

Amazing facts

It is sometimes difficult to comprehend the size of big numbers such as a million or a billion, but this can be made easier by considering the number in a familiar context as illustrated below:

● If you arranged a billion multilink cubes in a line they would extend halfway around the circumference of the Earth or, in other words, further than the distance from London to Sydney.

● If you covered an area with a billion multilink cubes they would take up more space than fifty football pitches.

● If your school hall is very large, say 30 metres long, 20 metres wide and 6 metres high, a billion multilink cubes would fill two of these halls and there would still be enough left over to fill your classroom.

● A billion seconds ago, none of the pupils in your school (and probably many of the staff) had not been born. Only those who have had their 31st birthday have lived for a billion seconds.

Common misconceptions

You now know about positive and negative powers, but what about a number, say 10, to the power zero? What is the value of 10^0? A common mistake is to think that the answer is zero, but if we use the pattern which exists in the powers of ten, first introduced on page 21, we will see that this is not the case. Here are the powers of ten from 3, decreasing to −3:

10^3	=	1000
10^2	=	100
10^1	=	10
10^0	=	?
10^{-1}	=	0.1
10^{-2}	=	0.01
10^{-3}	=	0.001

It is clear that each value is one-tenth of the value above, in other words as you work down the list you obtain the next value by dividing by ten (or by multiplying by ten if you are working up the list). The value of 10^0 must therefore be 1, not zero as many people think. In fact *any* number to the power zero gives an answer of 1.

This is also consistent with what was said earlier about the powers of ten corresponding to the place value column headings. The 'hundreds' column is represented by 10^2, the 'tens' column by 10^1 and the 'units' or 'ones' column by 10^0.

Teaching ideas

● Pupils in Year 6 could explore the patterns associated with powers in the same way as shown on pages 20 and 21.
● Powers of any number, in other words repeated multiplication, can be generated using the constant function of a calculator. For example, to produce powers of 5 use the following key presses:

| 5 | × | = | = | = |

Resources

A large number line displayed on the wall is an essential aid when teaching pupils of all ages about the structure of the number system. With very young pupils, a line with the numbers from zero to ten will be sufficient, but this will soon need to be extended to include bigger numbers. During Key Stage 2, appropriate number lines can be used to help pupils understand negative numbers and decimals. These sorts of number lines are available commercially, but you can also make your own easily for minimal cost.

In terms of commercially available paper-based resources, there are activities in the first chapters of *Further Curriculum Bank: Number* Key Stage 1 and *Further Curriculum Bank: Number* Key Stage 2, which focus on the structure of the number system and place value. Both books are published by Scholastic.

Chapter 2

Calculations

$$40 \div 5 = 8$$

$$72 + 151 = 223$$

To most people numeracy means calculations or the four rules of number, but this chapter aims to demonstrate that there is more to addition, subtraction, multiplication and division than you might at first think. Each of these basic operations can be thought of in different ways, there are important relationships between them, there are rules and conventions which need to be adhered to and there is a wealth of terminology associated with their use. All of these are considered in the following pages, along with an occasional dip into the history of mathematics.

The four rules of number

Subject facts

Addition
● Addition can b̲ [combining] two sets of objects and cou̲ [combining] five objects with t̲ [ ]ts and is written as $5 + 3 =$ [ ] on for the first time in this w̲

● Addition can be̲ [partitioning] a set of objects into two or more groups. This approach is more open-ended (because there is more than one way of doing it) and it also reinforces number bonds. Children are likely

Not happy about addition / partition more like divis

to use this approach when, for example, exploring the different ways of making ten.

● Addition can be linked to *counting*, when posing questions such as *What is three more than seven?* and also as a development of the combining approach. During early combining activities, pupils will count each set separately, record the numbers, combine the two sets, and then count them all again. Eventually they will be able to use one set (usually the larger one) as the starting point and count on from there.

Subtraction

● Subtraction is usually thought of as *removing* objects or *taking away*. For example, if you have nine sweets and eat four of them you will be left with five. This can be represented as $9 - 4 = 5$. This is the way that most pupils are introduced to the concept of subtraction.

● Subtraction can also be thought of in terms of the *difference* between two quantities. For example, if you have a strip of nine multilink cubes and a strip of four multilink cubes then the difference between them is 5. As before, this can be written as $9 - 4 = 5$, but in physical terms it is very different from the sweets situation. With the strips of multilink, nothing has been taken away and we are dealing with 13 objects, whereas with the sweets there were never more than nine objects under consideration and some of them were physically removed. The strips of multilink situation also illustrates the link between subtraction and counting since it can be tackled by either counting on from 4 (subtraction by *complementary addition*) or by counting back from 9. Not all pupils appreciate that counting forwards and counting backwards produces the same result.

Multiplication

● The usual way of considering multiplication is in terms of *lots of*. For example, if there are six eggs in a box then there will be 24 eggs in four boxes because four lots of six is 24. This is written as $4 \times 6 = 24$. Multiplication is clearly linked to addition, since many pupils in this situation will count on in sixes or think of it as $6 + 6 + 6 + 6 = 24$ (repeated addition).

Division

● Division can be thought of as *sharing*. For example, you might have 15 sweets which you want to share between three pupils. This can be done in a purely physical way without involving arithmetic at all. You simply distribute the sweets, one at a time, to each pupil in the same way that you would deal out a pack of cards. When translated into numbers and symbols this situation can be written as 15 ÷ 3 = 5, although many people will use the link with multiplication and think of it in terms of *Three times what equals fifteen?*

● Division can be thought of as *grouping*. For example you many sweets, each

r many sweets, each
c . Again, this can be done
i ng 3p, then removing
a e money has been used
u of *How many threes are*
th link between division
a many children will
ch ated addition) rather
th xample above, the
di ...... as 15 ÷ 3 = 5, but in physical terms sharing and grouping are very different. In a sharing situation you know the number of groups and want to work out how many will be in each one, whereas in a grouping situation you know the size of the group and want to know how many groups there will be.

multiply – repeated addition

division – repeated subtraction

Why you need to know these facts

It is important to be aware of the different ways of considering each of the four rules of number so that you can:

● Incorporate them into your planning and teaching. For example, you should provide addition activities which are based on partitioning as well as combining strategies.
● Offer alternative approaches to pupils who are struggling with a particular concept. For example, a child who is struggling with subtraction as 'taking away' may be able to cope more easily with the idea of 'difference' and therefore use counting on skills when subtracting.
● Equip pupils with a range of mental strategies from which they can select according to the numbers involved. For example, when subtracting two numbers which are close together it is better to think in terms of 'difference' and therefore count on from the lower number or back from the higher number. If the two numbers are far apart then it may be more efficient to view the problem in terms of 'removing'. Similarly, when dividing by a large number it is often better to think in terms of grouping using repeated subtraction, but this is not the case when dividing by a small number.

There is a wealth of mathematical language associated with calculations, and it is important that pupils are introduced to correct terminology at an appropriate age – indeed this is a major component of the National Numeracy Strategy. Traditionally, we have tended to shield pupils from what we think is complex mathematical terminology, but even very young pupils are happy to recite the names of dinosaurs such as Tyrannosaurus Rex, Diplodocus and Triceratops, so *divide* and *product* should hold no fears. As early as Reception pupils should be introduced to language such as *add, sum, total* and *take away*. By the end of Key Stage 1 this should be extended to include words such as *plus, subtract, multiply, divide* and *equals*. When they start Key Stage 2, pupils should be introduced to words such as *product* and *remainder*. The National Numeracy Strategy *Mathematical Vocabulary* book identifies the words and phrases that need to be introduced to pupils in each year of their primary education, so this should be consulted for additional guidance.

It is also important that the language you and your pupils use is grammatically, as well as mathematically, correct. Here are a few specific example to be aware of:

● Avoid the use of the word *sums* when you really mean *arithmetic*, as in *do the sums at the top of page seven*. Sum has a more specific meaning in the context of addition and so should only be used in this way. The expression *number sentence* is a better alternative and is identified as key language in the *Framework for Teaching Mathematics* from Year 1 onwards.

● Strictly speaking, the number sentence $5 + 3 = 8$ should be read as 'Five plus three equals eight'. *Add* is a widely used and acceptable alternative to *plus*.

● Similarly, read $5 - 3 = 2$ as 'Five minus three equals two'. *Subtract* and *take away* are acceptable alternatives to minus, although take away should be restricted to those situations which involve the physical removal of objects. Not all subtraction problems involve taking away and so this expression should not be overused.

● When reading number sentences use the word *equals* as an alternative to *makes, gives* or *leaves*. Equals can be used with all arithmetical operations, whereas these alternatives are only appropriate in particular contexts.

● Use the expression *multiplied by* rather than *times by* and avoid saying things such as *times it by five*. There is no such verb as 'to times'. When learning multiplication facts pupils are likely to come across language such as 'one times five is five, two times five is ten…'. Try to use the more correct and shorter alternative 'One five is five, two fives are ten…'.

● Avoid the expression *shared by*. The correct alternative is *divided by*. There is no reason why share cannot be used as long as it is used correctly, as in 'Share twelve sweets between three people', and only in situations which actually involve sharing.

● When doing division, avoid saying things such as *Two into eight goes four*. If you divide two objects into eight pieces then each piece will be one-quarter, not four. If the intended calculation is 'eight divided by two' then why not say so?

Amazing facts

● The *Crafte of Nombrynge*, written in about 1300, is one of the earliest manuscripts written in English that refers to mathematics. Here is a short extract:

> *"Here tells that ther ben 7 spices or partes of the craft. The first is called addicion, the secunde is called subtraccion. The thyrd is called duplacion. The 4 is called dimydicion. The 5 is called multiplicacion. The 6 is called dyuision. The 7 is called extraccion of the rote."*

Can you work out what addicion, subtraccion, duplacion, dimydicion, multiplicacion, dyuision and extraccion of the rote are referring to? They are addition, subtraction, doubling, halving, multiplication, division and the calculating of roots (for example square roots).

● The word 'plus' is short for 'surplus' and its use originates from European warehouses during medieval times where sacks, crates and barrels were marked with a '+' or a '–' to indicate whether they were above or below their intended weight.

Common misconceptions

Multiplication by 10, 100, 1000, and so on.
Everyone knows how to do this. All you do is 'add a nought' or 'stick a couple of noughts on the end'. But we have to be careful when we provide pupils with rules which only work in certain circumstances and which do not help to reinforce basic number concepts. The popular rules for multiplying by powers of ten are good examples of this malpractice. Adding a zero is fine when you are working with whole numbers, but is not appropriate when decimals are involved. For example, if you want to multiply 2.5 by 10 you clearly do not place a zero on the end or indeed anywhere else. A far better way of explaining this to pupils is in terms of the digits moving left into another column.

The diagram below illustrates this process for 43 × 100:

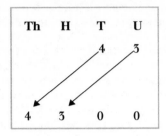

This method can be used for whole numbers and decimals, it reinforces work on place value and it can be adapted for division by 10, 100, 1000 and so on.

Division by zero.

Zero tends to cause problems for many pupils. For example, they are not always quick to appreciate that zero has no effect when it is added to, subtracted from or multiplied by a number. But it is not just pupils who have trouble with zero. Do you know what happens if you divide by zero? What is the answer to 8 ÷ 0? Ask your colleagues in school and see what they think. A common mistake is to think that the answer is zero, but in fact the answer is infinite or undefined. Use a calculator to work out the answer to 8 ÷ 0 and see what happens. You should get an error message because the calculator is unable to display an infinitely large number. But why is the answer infinite? The pattern below, in which 8 is divided by a smaller and smaller number each time, should help you to understand:

8 ÷ 4	=	2
8 ÷ 2	=	4
8 ÷ 1	=	8
8 ÷ 0.5	=	16
8 ÷ 0.25	=	32
8 ÷ 0.1	=	80
8 ÷ 0.05	=	160
8 ÷ 0.01	=	800
8 ÷ 0.001	=	8000
8 ÷ 0.0001	=	80000

As the number you are dividing by (the divisor) gets closer and closer to zero, the answer gets larger and larger. If this pattern was continued so that eventually you were, in effect, dividing by zero, the answer would be infinitely large.

Always emphasize the connections between the four arithmetical operations. For example, after combining two sets of objects during addition activities you could ask questions such as *How many will I have if I take this set away?* and then separate the two sets you have just combined. There is no reason at all why addition and subtraction should be taught separately, indeed this can sometimes hinder pupils' ability to see the relationship between the two operations. Similarly, it is important to stress the links between multiplication and addition, between multiplication and division, and between division and subtraction.

Key concepts, laws and convention

Inverse operations
An *inverse operation* is one which undoes (or reverses) the effect of the original operation. For example, subtraction is the inverse of addition because if you add 3 and then subtract 3 you will be back where you started. It follows that addition is the inverse of subtraction and similarly multiplication and division are the inverse of one another. Another pair of operations for which this is true is squaring and taking the square root.

Using brackets
Brackets are used to denote precedence when doing calculations, in other words anything in brackets must be worked out first, as illustrated in the examples below:

$2 + (3 \times 4) = 14$	Work out 3×4 first and then add the answer to 2.
$(2 + 3) \times 4 = 20$	Work out $2 + 3$ first and then multiply the answer by 4.

$(2 + 3) \times (4 + 5) = 45$ Work out the answer in each set of brackets and then multiply the two answers.

Commutative law

An operation involving two numbers is commutative if the order in which the two numbers are used does not affect the result, as illustrated by the examples below:

$8 + 5 = 5 + 8$ Addition is commutative.

$4 - 7 \neq 7 - 4$ Subtraction is not commutative.

$2 \times 9 = 9 \times 2$ Multiplication is commutative.

$6 \div 3 \neq 3 \div 6$ Division is not commutative.

Associative law

This is an extension of the commutative law for situations involving three or more numbers. If the order in which the operation is applied to the numbers does not affect the result then the operation is associative. This is illustrated in the examples below, the brackets indicating the order in which the calculations are to be carried out:

$(3 + 5) + 7 = 3 + (5 + 7)$ Addition is associative.

$(8 - 6) - 4 \neq 8 - (6 - 4)$ Subtraction is not associative.

$(2 \times 3) \times 4 = 2 \times (3 \times 4)$ Multiplication is associative.

$(8 \div 4) \div 2 \neq 8 \div (4 \div 2)$ Division is not associative.

Distributive law

The distributive law involves the use of two operations and at least three numbers. It provides slightly different, but equivalent, forms of a particular number sentence. Here is an example involving multiplication and addition:

$5 \times (3 + 7) = (5 \times 3) + (5 \times 7)$ Multiplication is distributive over addition.

Further examples involving other pairs of operations are shown below:

$4 \times (8 - 3) = (4 \times 8) - (4 \times 3)$ Multiplication is distributive over subtraction.

$$(5 + 4) \div 3 = (5 \div 3) + (4 \div 3)$$

Division is distributive over addition.

$$3 = 1^2/_3 + 1\,^1/_3 = 3$$

$$(9 - 1) \div 4 = (9 \div 4) - (1 \div 4)$$

Division is distributive over subtraction.

$$2 = 2^1/_4 - \,^1/_4$$

Equivalence

When working mentally, it is often beneficial to replace one relatively complex calculation with two or more equivalent ones which make the overall process easier, as illustrated by the examples below:

● Multiply by four or eight by a process of repeated doubling.

● Multiply by five by first multiplying by ten and then halving.

● Multiplying by nine by first multiplying by ten and then subtracting.

Sometimes it is only necessary to do a single equivalent calculation as shown in these two examples.

● If, when doing a subtraction, you increase or decrease both numbers by the same amount, this does not affect the answer. For example, the difference between 28 and 45 is the same as the difference between 30 and 47. Increasing the original numbers by two produces an easier equivalent calculation.

● If, when dividing, you change both numbers by a certain scale factor (ie multiply or divide by the same amount), then this again does not affect the answer. For example, the calculation $48\,000 \div 1200$ is equivalent to the easier $480 \div 12$ (both numbers have been divided by 100). Similarly, $2.7 \div 0.3$ is equivalent to $27 \div 3$ (both numbers have been multiplied by 10).

It is not just calculations which have equivalent forms; sometimes it is beneficial to work with the numbers themselves in an alternative but equivalent form, for example, the number 746 can be thought of as $700 + 40 + 6$.

Tests for divisibility

These allow you to quickly check whether a given number is divisible by other numbers. Here are the most commonly known tests:

Divisible by	Test
2	Last digit is 0, 2, 4, 6 or 8.
3	Add the digits; add the digits of the answer; repeat until you get a single digit which should be 3, 6 or 9.
4	Number formed by the last two digits is a multiple of 4.
5	Last digit is 5 or 0.
6	These are even multiples of 3 so check that the tests for 2 and 3 above both work.
7	There is no simple test.
8	Number formed by the last three digits is a multiple of 8.
9	Add the digits; add the digits of the answer; repeat until you get a single digit which should be 9.
10	Last digit is 0.
11	Working from right to left, alternately subtract and add the digits. If the final answer is divisible by 11 then so is the original number.
12	These are divisible by both 3 and 4 so check that these tests both work.

Inverses

Understanding the inverse relationships that exist between pairs of operations is essential in order to calculate efficiently and also to check the results of your calculations. You will also need to make pupils aware of this important concept from an early age as indicated by the following examples.

Why you need to know these facts

By the end of Key Stage 1 pupils should:
● begin to understand that addition reverses subtraction
● be able to say or write the subtraction fact corresponding to a given addition fact and vice versa
● understand and use the principle that doubling reverses halving
● begin to understand the principle that multiplication reverses division.

During the early part of Key Stage 2 pupils should:
● be able to say or write a division statement corresponding to a given multiplication statement
● be able to check subtraction with addition, check halving with doubling and check division with multiplication
● use, read and write the word 'inverse'.

Brackets
When calculations become more complex, involving two or more operations, brackets remove any uncertainty or ambiguity about the order in which the calculations must be carried out. Pupils should start to use brackets in their number work during Year 5 and this will provide a firm foundation for algebra at Key Stage 3 which makes extensive use of brackets.

Commutative, Associative and Distributive Laws
These laws form the foundation of all arithmetic and so an understanding of them is absolutely vital. They do not need to be known in any formal way, indeed it is not even necessary for pupils to know them by name, but what is needed is an ability to use and apply them to make methods of calculations more efficient. They also lie at the heart of much of the algebra work pupils will encounter during Key Stage 3.

The following examples indicate the opportunities pupils will have, from an early age, to develop an understanding of these laws and to use them in their number work.
By the end of Key Stage 1 pupils should:
● be able to put the larger number first in order to count on
● understand that $5 + 2 = 2 + 5$ but that $5 - 2$ is not the same as $2 - 5$
● understand that $5 + 2 + 6 = (5 + 2) + 6 = 5 + (2 + 6)$
● be able to add three numbers by using strategies such as looking for pairs that make ten and doing these first, or starting with the largest
● check by repeating addition in a different order
● begin to recognize that multiplication can be done in any order.
During the early part of Key Stage 2 pupils should:
● check by repeating multiplication in a different order
● understand that $16 \div 2$ is not the same as $2 \div 16$
● be able to partition and use the distributive law, for instance $32 \times 3 = (30 \times 3) + (2 \times 3)$
● understand, and use when appropriate, the principles (but not the names) of the commutative, associative and distributive laws as they apply to multiplication.

Equivalence

Being able to recognize that a number or a calculation can be written in a more manageable way will enable efficient calculation strategies to be developed and used. This concept of equivalence needs to be introduced even during Key Stage 1. For example, pupils will start to partition two-digit numbers into tens and units, or they will add nine by first adding ten and then subtracting one. This early use of equivalent numbers and equivalent calculations needs to be developed and extended throughout Key Stage 2.

Tests for divisibility

These are a powerful aid, not only when doing division, but also when checking multiplication answers and working with factors and multiples (see page 46). As early as Year 2 pupils should recognize that multiples of ten end in a zero, that multiples of five end in zero or five, and that multiples of two have an even units digit. In Year 3 this should be extended to include checks for divisibility by 100 (last two digits are zeros) and 50 (last two digits are 50 or 00). This repertoire of tests needs to be extended during Key Stage 2 so that by Year 6 pupils are able to use all of those shown on page 35. Pupils do not need to be introduced to the terms *divisible* and *divisibility* until Year 5.

Vocabulary

As with all aspects of mathematics, do not be afraid to introduce pupils to the formal language associated with a new concept. Most pupils are more than capable of coping with new terminology, although sometimes you might need to use a range of vocabulary to help pupils understand it. For example, pupils in the middle of KS2 should be introduced to the expression *inverse* which could be explained in terms of 'opposite', 'reverses' or 'undoes'.

Amazing facts

● The tests for divisibility by the numbers 2 to 12 were widely known and used right up until the beginning of the 17th century. Decimal notation had not been introduced at this time and so the tests for divisibility were very useful when cancelling down fractions involving large numerators and denominators.
● Write down any two-digit number (for example 38) and repeat it three times to produce a six-digit number (383838). This number will always be divisible by 7. Try it for yourself, or try it with your pupils.
● Write down any three-digit number which comprises

three different digits (for example 724). Repeat the digits to produce a six-digit number (724724). Divide the six-digit number by 7 (don't worry about remainders – there won't be any). Then divide the answer by 11 (again, there will definitely be no remainder). Finally divide the answer by 13 (you've guessed it – no remainder) and you should be left with your original three-digit number. Truly amazing!

Common misconceptions

One automatically thinks that an inverse operation must be different to the operation it is undoing but this is not always the case. The inverse of the operation *work out the reciprocal* (see page 20 in Chapter 1) is *work out the reciprocal*; in other words this operation is its own inverse. For example, the reciprocal of 2 is ½ and the reciprocal of ½ is 2. You simply repeat the original operation to get back to the starting number.

Teaching ideas

Inverses

Help pupils to develop an understanding of inverses during a mental practice session by asking questions such as *I've thought of a number, doubled it and added five. My answer is eleven. What was my original number?*

You could explain situations such as this with the aid of two flow diagrams. The first one illustrates the calculations you have carried out to get the answer 11. The second one works backwards from 11, doing the inverse operation each time.

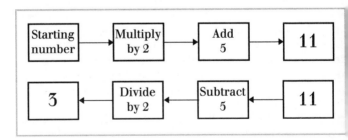

Brackets

Write $3 + 4 \times 5$ on the board and ask pupils to work out the answer. Most are likely to say 35, but some might suggest 23. This provides a nice way of introducing the idea of brackets to denote precedence. Also demonstrate the working out of the answer using two electronic calculators which produce different answers. Some calculators will give the answer 35 while others will give 23.

Equivalence

At the upper end of Key Stage 2, use 'broken keys' calculator activities to develop children's understanding of the relationships between the four operations and the notion of equivalence. In these sorts of activities, restrictions are placed on the calculator keys that can be used because they are 'broken'. Pose questions such as:
● Work out 47 ÷ 13 (correct to three decimal places) without using the division key.
● Work out 3.75 × 2.816 without using the multiplication key.
● Work out 4.9 × 1.35 without using the decimal point key.
The first question requires an understanding of multiplication as the inverse of division and an ability to use trial and improvement methods.

The second question could be tackled by firstly using repeated addition to get three lots of 2.816. Then use division to get one-quarter of 2.816 and finally repeated addition (possibly using the calculator constant function) to get three-quarters. An ability to use the memory facility of the calculator is also very useful.

The third question could be tackled by working out 49 × 135 and placing the decimal point correctly in the answer using estimating skills.

Approaches to calculation

Below is a summary of the key points regarding the development of calculating methods:

Subject facts

● The results of some calculations eventually become memorized facts which can be recalled instantly – for example addition, subtraction and multiplication facts, halves and doubles.
● Known number facts can be used to derive others which cannot be recalled instantly, for example a knowledge of doubles up to 10 can be used to quickly work out 40 + 40.
● Mental calculations should always be seen as a first resort when tackling a problem.
● There is always more than one way of approaching any given calculation and so the choice of mental strategy will vary according to personal preference and the numbers involved.
● Mental methods need to be taught, discussed and compared. It should not be assumed that all pupils will be

capable of devising a range of methods to cope with different circumstances.

● The ability to carry out efficient mental calculations is based on a sound knowledge of number facts and an understanding of place value.

● The use of mental methods does not mean that nothing is written down. The numbers used to produce the answer, as well as the answer itself, often need to be recorded on paper, and in some cases informal jottings are necessary because it is not possible to remember the results of intermediate calculations.

● Mental skills need to be practised regularly, even when they have been mastered and the pupil has moved on to use other approaches.

● The temptation to introduce pencil and paper methods too early should be avoided. Pupils need to have developed sound mental skills and a knowledge of number facts before moving on to pencil and paper approaches.

● Pencil and paper methods are often based on mental methods and so are varied and personal.

● As is the case with mental strategies, pencil and paper methods need to be taught, discussed and compared.

● The traditional pencil and paper methods, for example subtraction by decomposition, are often very efficient, but should still be viewed as just one possible way of doing the calculation.

● There are some situations where the use of an electronic calculator is the most appropriate approach, for example when the calculations or the numbers involved are too complex to deal with using mental or written methods.

● The whole purpose of learning various methods of calculation is so that they can be used and applied. It is therefore important that pupils are given opportunities to practise their calculating skills in a wide range of contexts, to solve real-life number problems and to engage in open-ended and investigative number work.

Why you need to know these facts

The key points identified above are the basic principles which underlie the approaches to calculation suggested in the National Numeracy Strategy documentation. You have probably heard all of these basic principles before, but they have been emphasized here because they really are crucial and because for many schools and teachers they represent a shift away from the approaches that have been used in the past. Up until now the curriculum has not placed sufficient emphasis on mental calculations, other than the recall of number bonds and multiplication tables, and this has usually been at the expense of excessive concentration on the traditional pencil and paper routines which have been introduced far too early, before mental skills have fully developed. The electronic calculator has often been blamed for primary pupils' poor numeracy skills but there is no evidence to support this; in fact there is much evidence which suggests that calculators are not used to the extent that many commentators would lead us to believe. It is the balance between mental methods and traditional pencil and paper methods which we have been getting wrong in the past, not the balance between mental methods and calculator methods. By adhering to the basic principles identified above, this imbalance should be redressed.

Vocabulary

The key language and vocabulary issues associated with calculations have already been discussed earlier in this chapter on page 29.

In addition, please refer to the National Numeracy Strategy *Mathematical Vocabulary* book which identifies the words and phrases that need to be introduced to pupils during each year of their primary education. These are organized under appropriate headings, including one for vocabulary associated with calculations.

A brief history of calculating methods

Amazing facts

The Egyptians, the Greeks, the Romans, the Chinese and even Europeans in the Middle Ages all calculated on abacuses or something similar. These devices are based on place value, with columns for units, tens, hundreds and so on, and they make use of zero by simply not having any beads in a particular column. However, despite having a calculating system based on place value, all of these people used a clumsy notational system which lacked both place value and zero. It was therefore impossible to do pencil and paper arithmetic as we do today. Our present system of denoting numbers using the digits 0 to 9 developed from the Hindu-Arabic system and was introduced to Europe by Fibonacci in the 13th century. It was only then that pencil and paper arithmetic as we know it became possible, resulting in a bitter struggle between the 'Abacists' and the 'Algorists'. Calculating by 'algorism' was forbidden by law in some European countries and so had to be done behind locked doors. It was only in the 16th century when paper became plentiful that the new notation and methods of calculating became widely accepted and the abacus slowly disappeared. However, an abacus-type system of notched sticks was still used in the House of Commons for the Exchequer accounts right up until the early 19th century when it was finally replaced by pencil and paper methods.

Amazing additions and subtractions

Write down any number which comprises three different digits.	492
Reverse the digits to produce a second number.	294
Subtract the smaller number from the larger.	492 – 294 = 198
Reverse the digits of the answer and add to the answer.	891 + 198 = 1089
The answer is always 1089.	

Try it for yourself or with your pupils.

Amazing doubles

Repeated doubling is a technique for multiplication which pupils should be made aware of. You might like to discuss this amazing repeated doubling situation with your pupils.

Suppose you were to tear an ordinary sheet of paper in half, place the two pieces on top of one another, tear them in half again, place the pieces on top of one another, and so on. If you were to make fifty tears altogether (not physically possible, but let's imagine that it is), how tall would the final pile of paper be? Ask your pupils what they think the answer is. You might be amazed to know that the pile would be 112 million kilometres high, or, if you prefer, 70 million miles! You don't believe it? Well let's work it out. A typical ream of 500 sheets of A4 paper is 5cm thick, which means that the thickness of each sheet is about 0.1mm. If you double this fifty times it works out to be 112 million kilometres. If you don't fancy all of this tearing you could stop after only ten tears when the pile will be about 10cm tall, or after twenty tears when it will be just over 100 metres tall, or after thirty tears when it will have grown to over 100 km tall or after forty tears when it will be about 110 000 km tall.

This situation is not dissimilar to the well-known legend about the Shah of Persia who was so impressed by the game of chess that he asked its inventor to name his reward. The shrewd inventor, who was probably a mathematician, asked for one grain of rice to be placed on the first square of a chessboard, two grains on the second, four grains on the third, eight grains on the fourth, and so on until all 64 squares had been used. The Shah of Persia thought that this was a meagre reward and so agreed, without thinking through the consequences. The total amount of rice involved is in fact greater than the world's annual production of grain today!

Amazing multiplication

Traditional pencil and paper methods for multiplication are based on a knowledge of multiplication facts up to 10 × 10, but how would you like to try a method which requires nothing more than doubling and halving? This ancient method is demonstrated below in working out the answer to 57 × 35:

57	35	Write down the two numbers.
~~28~~	~~70~~	Halve the number on the left, ignoring any remainder, and double the number on the right.
~~14~~	~~140~~	
7	280	Repeat, but stop when the number on the left is 1.
3	560	Cross out all lines in which the number on the left is even.
1	1120	
	1995	Add up the remaining numbers on the right.

You might like to try this ancient method of multiplication with your pupils.

It is a common belief that the traditional pencil and paper routines are the 'correct' way of doing a calculation, but they are certainly not the only way and in fact they are often not the quickest or most efficient approach to adopt, as illustrated by the following examples:

Common misconceptions

Example 1: 4003 – 3998
It makes no sense at all to tackle this question using subtraction by decomposition, but it is a sad fact that many pupils are forced to use this method when faced with

numbers such as these. The zeros in the first number often cause all sorts of problems and so many pupils get the answer wrong. A more efficient approach is to recognise that the two numbers are close together and so mentally count on from the lower number.

Example 2: 199 × 4

Again, many pupils would choose to use the traditional pencil and paper method for multiplication because this is the only approach they have been taught. It would be far quicker to mentally work out 4 × 200 and then subtract 4 from the answer.

These two examples demonstrate that we must examine critically the efficiency and appropriateness of traditional pencil and paper methods, and this in turn has implications for the ways in which we teach pupils to carry out calculations. There is a place for the traditional routines but we must acknowledge that in certain situations there are better alternatives.

Teaching ideas

A key point which has already been made earlier in this chapter is that pupils should encounter a variety of calculating methods, not just the traditional ones. Here are a few alternatives that you could try with your pupils:

Example 1: Work out 289 + 344

```
      289
   +  344
      500     Say 200 plus 300 rather than 2 plus 3
      120     Say 80 plus 40 rather than 8 plus 4
   +   13
      633     Add the three answers mentally
```

The same working could be set out horizontally as shown below:

$$289 + 344 = (200 + 80 + 9) + (300 + 40 + 4)$$
$$= 500 + 120 + 13$$
$$= 633$$

These sorts of approaches build on the mental methods pupils have been taught already and they are based on an understanding of the number system and place value.

Example 2: Work out 417 – 263
Mental subtraction is often done by counting on from the
lower number so why not use the same approach when
dealing with larger numbers on paper?

```
263

        + 7    Count on 7 from 263 to get to 270
270

        + 30   Count on 30 from 270 to get to 300
300

        +100   Count on 100 from 300 to get to 400
400

        + 17   Count on 17 from 400 to get to 417
417
        ___
        154    Add the four steps mentally
```

Again, this method builds on pupils' previous knowledge
and experience, and is based on understanding rather than
the ability to remember a set of instructions. The traditional
methods for pencil and paper subtraction, for example by
decomposition ('borrowing') are fine as long as pupils can
remember the procedure and carry it out accurately. But
because these traditional routines are based on memory
rather than on understanding, there are always going to be
some pupils who simply forget or get it wrong.

Example 3: Work out 125 × 52
This tabular or grid approach to long multiplication builds
on pupils' understanding of place value and on their ability
to multiply mentally by 10, 100 and multiples of these.

×	100	20	5	Totals
50	5000	1000	250	6250
2	200	40	10	250
				6500

In the example above, row totals have been calculated and
then added together to give the final answer, 6500. A
variation would be to calculate the three column totals
(5200, 1040 and 260) and then add these together. Which
approach is adopted will depend on personal choice.

These are just three possible examples of non-traditional calculating methods which can be adapted in various ways. The *Framework for Teaching Mathematics* provides more detailed guidance on the many approaches to mental as well as pencil and paper calculations as well as the effective use of electronic calculators.

Special numbers associated with calculations

Subject facts

Multiples

These are the answers in the multiplication tables or multiplication facts. For example, the multiples of twelve are 12, 24, 36, 48 and so on.

Lowest Common Multiple (LCM)

The multiples of three are 3, 6, 9, 12, 15, 18...
The multiples of five are 5, 10, 15, 20, 25, 30...
The common multiples of three and five are 15, 30, 45...
The lowest common multiple of three and five is 15 – in other words the lowest number which is a multiple of both three and five.

Factors

A number can be divided by each of its factors without leaving a remainder. The factors must be whole numbers. For example, the factors of twelve are 1, 2, 3, 4, 6 and 12 because twelve is divisible by each of these without leaving a remainder. Factors always come as a pair of numbers (often called a *factor pair*) which when multiplied are equal to the number under consideration, so in this example the factor pairs are 1 and 12, 2 and 6, 3 and 4.

Prime numbers

A prime number is divisible only by itself and one, in other words it has exactly two factors. The prime numbers less than 20 are 2, 3, 5, 7, 11, 13, 17 and 19.

Composite numbers

These have more than two factors, in other words they are the non-prime numbers (with the exception of zero and one which are neither prime nor composite).

Product of prime factors

Any number can be expressed as the product of its prime factors. Start by identifying a factor pair for the number concerned. Then express each of the factors as the product of two of its own factors. Repeat this process until all of the factors are prime numbers. The example below shows how the number 120 can be expressed as the product of prime factors:

$120 = 4 \times 30$		Start by multiplying a factor pair.
$= 2 \times 2 \times 30$		4 can be written as 2×2.
$= 2 \times 2 \times 5 \times 6$		30 can be written as 5×6.
$= 2 \times 2 \times 5 \times 2 \times 3$		6 can be written as 2×3.
$= 2 \times 2 \times 2 \times 3 \times 5$		Stop when all factors are prime.

Square numbers

A square number is produced when any whole number is multiplied by itself. For example, 36 is a square number because $6 \times 6 = 36$. When we multiply any number by itself we say we are *squaring* it and, in the case of 6×6, we often say 'six squared' and can write it as 6^2:

$$6^2 = 6 \times 6 = 36$$

Square numbers can be illustrated as squares on a grid and also as arrangements of dots as shown below:

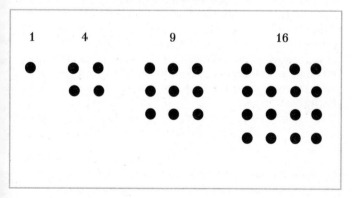

Square roots

Finding the square root of a number is the inverse of squaring. For example the square root of 36 is 6 because 6 squared is 36. The mathematical symbol used to denote square root is $\sqrt{}$ as shown in the examples below:

$$\sqrt{9} = 3$$
$$\sqrt{64} = 8$$
$$\sqrt{100} = 10$$
$$\sqrt{30} = 5.477 \text{ (to three decimal places)}$$

Triangular numbers

The easiest way to explain triangular numbers is with the aid of arrangements of dots as shown in the diagram below:

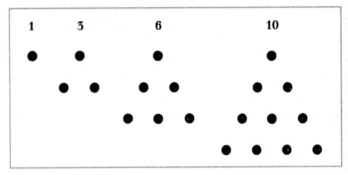

The 5th triangular number is $10 + 5 = 15$.
The 6th triangular number is $15 + 6 = 21$.
The 7th triangular number is $21 + 7 = 28$.
The 8th triangular number is $28 + 8 = 36$.

Cube numbers

A cube number is produced when any whole number is multiplied by itself and then by itself again, for example 125 is a cube number because $5 \times 5 \times 5 = 125$. When carrying out this process we often say 'five cubed' and can write it down as 5^3:

$$5^3 = 5 \times 5 \times 5 = 125$$

Square numbers can represented by two-dimensional arrangements of squares. In a similar fashion, cube numbers can be represented by three-dimensional arrangements of cubes as shown opposite.

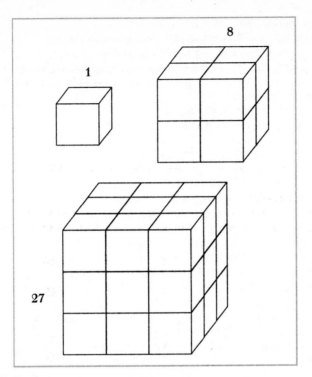

Cube roots

There is an inverse relationship between cubing and finding the cube root in the same way that there is an inverse relationship between squaring and finding the square root. For example, the cube root of 125 is 5 because 5 cubed is 125. The notation for this and other examples is illustrated below:

$$\sqrt[3]{125} = 5$$
$$\sqrt[3]{64} = 4$$
$$\sqrt[3]{1000} = 10$$
$$\sqrt[3]{100} = 4.642 \text{ (to three decimal places)}$$

If you want to be able to use, apply and explore mathematics then you need to know and understand the language of mathematics. All of the special qualities described above are key aspects of mathematical terminology which you need to be familiar with because they will feature in your teaching at both Key Stage 1 and

Why you need to know these facts

Key Stage 2 as indicated by the following examples:
By the end of Key Stage 1 pupils should be able to
● understand and begin to use *multiple*.
Towards the end of Key Stage 2 pupils should be able to:
● find the smallest number that is a common multiple of two numbers
● use, read and write *factor*
● use, read and write *prime* and *prime factor*
● find all the prime factors of any number up to 100
● use, read and write *square number*
In addition they lay the foundation for work at Key Stage 3 as illustrated by the following examples:
● An understanding of *lowest common multiple* is essential when ordering, adding or subtracting fractions because these require the use of a common denominator which is, in effect, the lowest common multiple.
● Familiarity with terms such as *square root, cube number* and *cube root* is not required until Key Stage 3 but there is no reason why they cannot be introduced to many pupils before leaving primary school.

Furthermore, they contribute to the development of your own subject knowledge, thus enabling you to understand mathematical terminology that you may come across in mathematics textbooks or journals and respond to challenging questions posed by able pupils or colleagues in school. For example, you might be asked to explain what the $\sqrt[3]{\ }$ key on an electronic calculator is used for.

Vocabulary

As always, ensure that pupils are introduced to the correct terminology as soon as they encounter a new mathematical concept. Expressions such as *multiple, factor, prime, prime factor* and *square number* should be familiar vocabulary to pupils by the time they leave primary school. Exactly when pupils should be introduced to each of these is considered in the 'Why you need to know these facts' section above.

Don't confuse factors with *factorials*. An exclamation mark is used as an abbreviation for factorials, for example 4!, which is read as 'factorial four' or 'four factorial' (both are perfectly acceptable). The meaning of this is demonstrated below:

$$4! = 4 \times 3 \times 2 \times 1 = 24$$

Factorials are used in situations which involve combinations, for example, four books can be arranged on a shelf in 4! = 24 different ways.

Triangular and square numbers

The ancient Greeks had no number symbols and so represented whole numbers using pebbles placed in the sand. By arranging the pebbles in a particular way they became aware of triangular and square numbers. Did you know that the Latin word for pebble is *calculus*, as in calculate and calculation?

The sum of any two consecutive triangular numbers is always a square number, for example 3 + 6 = 9 and 6 + 10 = 16. Try it yourself with two bigger consecutive triangular numbers.

This can be explained by first illustrating triangular numbers as squares rather than as dots:

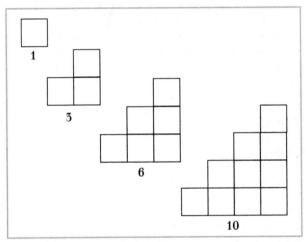

Any two consecutive arrangements can be fitted together to form a square as shown below:

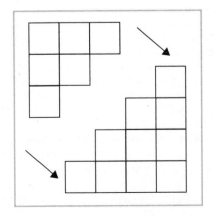

Perfect numbers

The ancient Greeks classified whole numbers as odd or even and as prime or composite, but they also classified them as *defective, excessive* or *perfect*. A defective number is one which is less than the sum of its factors (not including itself as a factor). For example, the factors of 12 (excluding itself) are 1, 2, 3, 4 and 6, and the sum of these factors is 16. An excessive number is one that is greater than the sum of its factors, for example, the factors of 14 are 1, 2 and 7 which have a sum of only 10. A number which is the same as the sum of its factors is perfect, for example the number 6 is perfect.

As part of their work on factors, you could ask your pupils to classify numbers as defective, excessive or perfect. The first four perfect numbers are 6, 28, 496 and 8128. You might like to check this for yourself by finding the sum of all their factors. If you have plenty of time on your hands you could also do this for the fifth perfect number, 33 550 336.

Prime numbers

On a 100-square, shade all of the multiples of six then, using a different colour, shade all of the prime numbers. What do you notice? Amazing isn't it? I wonder if this is the case with prime numbers beyond 100?

It is possible to generate prime numbers using the formula $P = n^2 + n + 11$. By substituting each of the numbers from 1 to 9 in place of n you will get prime values for P. For example, when $n = 1$, $P = (1)^2 + 1 + 11 = 13$ which is prime. Try using values of n from 2 to 9 to generate other prime numbers.

Similarly, the formula $P = n^2 - n + 41$ will generate prime numbers when each of the numbers from 1 to 40 is substituted in place of n. Try using this formula to generate prime numbers less than 100.

Can a number have an odd number of factors?

Factors always come as factor pairs and so it is tempting to think that all numbers must have an even number of factors. Can you think of a number which has an odd number of factors? How about a square number, for example 16? All of the factors come in pairs (1 × 16, 2 × 8 and 4 × 4), but one of them is an identical pair. All square numbers therefore have an odd number of factors.

Is 1 prime?

There is sometimes confusion over whether or not zero and

one are prime numbers. You would not be alone in thinking that one is the first prime number, but if you apply the definition provided on page 46, there should be no confusion. A prime number has exactly two factors and so zero and one are not prime because the former has no factors and the latter has only one.

Factors

Pupils can practise finding factors using factor trees. The diagram below shows two possible factor trees for 24:

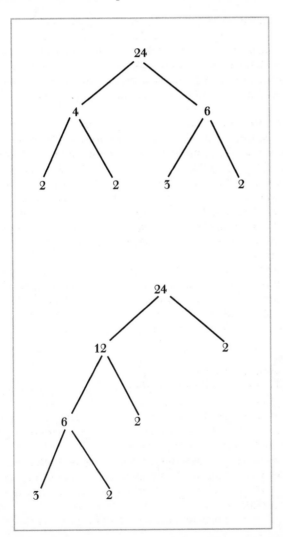

Start by identifying a factor pair and then split each of the two numbers into another factor pair. Do not use a factor pair which includes 1. For example, do not split 2 into the factor pair 2 × 1 because this process could be continued endlessly (this is an important point which should be discussed with pupils).

The two trees look different, but notice that the number of end-points is the same on both and the numbers at the end-points are the same (2, 2, 2 and 3). As a check, the numbers at the end-points can be multiplied and should produce the starting number (ie $2 \times 2 \times 2 \times 3 = 24$).

Prime numbers

The factor trees above provide one possible way of introducing the idea of a prime number since the numbers at the end points are all prime. The trees can also be used to express a number as the product of prime factors since the numbers at the end-points multiply to give the starting number.

An alternative investigative approach for introducing prime numbers is by drawing or shading rectangles on squared paper. Ten of the squares on the paper can be shaded to form a 5 × 2 rectangle. Similarly, nine squares can be shaded to form a 3 × 3 square (a square is a special rectangle). Pupils could investigate for which numbers of squares it is possible to form rectangles and for which numbers it is not (a rectangle of width 1 does not count). The numbers for which it cannot be done are prime numbers.

Another way of thinking of prime numbers is as those numbers which do not appear on a multiplication tables grid, other than in the first row or first column (ie the multiples of 1).

Resources

The following resources are invaluable in the development of effective approaches to calculation among pupils in the primary school:
● Sets of objects such as multilink cubes or counters are essential items for pupils to have access to in the early stages when they are developing an understanding of each arithmetical operation.
● A large number line displayed on the classroom wall to

assist the development of counting on and counting back skills, as part of addition and subtraction work.

● A large 100-square displayed on the classroom wall to enable pupils to spot patterns when counting on and counting back in tens starting at any number, as part of addition and subtraction work, and also to assist the learning of multiplication facts.

● A large multiplication tables grid displayed on the classroom wall as a teaching aid when considering special numbers such as multiples, square numbers, prime numbers and so on.

● 0–9 digit cards for individual pupils to use to hold up their answers to questions posed during mental practice sessions.

● HTU cards to help pupils develop an understanding of place value by partitioning a number into its constituent parts and using this to develop strategies for mental calculations.

Photocopiable sheets to produce resources such as these, together with suggestions for using them in the classroom, can be found in the following Scholastic books: *Further Curriculum Bank: Number* Key Stage 1 and *Further Curriculum Bank: Number* Key Stage 2.

An excellent piece of software which can be used by the teacher with whole classes of pupils is *Counting Machine*. This can be used with young pupils to introduce and reinforce the structure of the number system, counting on, counting back, and so on, but can also be used with older pupils to investigate number sequences, multiples, square numbers, triangular numbers and so on. It is available from:

Numeracy Software Solutions
PO Box 533
Hull
HU5 4YN
sales@numeracy.karoo.co.uk

Various packs of software, covering themes such as A Sense of Number, Properties of Number, Numeracy and Co-ordinates are available from SMILE Mathematics at the following address:

SMILE Mathematics
Isaac Newton Centre
108A Lancaster Road
London
W11 1QS
www.rmplc.co.uk/orgs/smile

Chapter 3

Fractions, decimals, percentages & ratios

The mere thought of having to solve problems involving fractions, decimals, percentages and ratios strikes fear into the hearts of many adults let alone children in primary schools. Wouldn't life be so much easier if we only had to contend with integers? Perhaps it would, but unfortunately there is no way of avoiding these ways of representing numbers and quantities because they feature so strongly in many aspects of the real world. It is therefore important that everyone understands and is able to work effectively with fractions, decimals, percentages and ratios in the ways outlined in this chapter.

Language and notation

Subject facts

Fractions

In the past, the expression *vulgar fractions* was often used to distinguish them from *decimal fractions* although today we tend to simply say 'fraction' and 'decimal'.

The following examples illustrate the different sorts of fractions you are likely to come across:

$$\frac{3}{8} \qquad \frac{5}{2} \qquad 3\frac{1}{4}$$

The first example is a *proper fraction*, that is, a fraction which is less than 1. The top and bottom numbers in all fractions are called the *numerator* and *denominator* respectively. The numerator in a proper fraction is always less than the denominator.

The second example is an *improper fraction* because the numerator is bigger than the denominator, indicating a number which is greater than 1. These are often called *top-heavy* fractions. An improper fraction can be converted into a mixed number (see below) although often it is appropriate to leave it as it is, for example when multiplying fractions.

The final example is a *mixed number* because it comprises a mixture of whole numbers and fractional parts.

Decimals

Decimal notation is simply an extension of the place value system used for whole numbers. The column headings for whole numbers such as hundreds, tens and units, are all powers of ten, with each heading being one-tenth of the previous one as you move from left to right. Continue this beyond the units to get tenths, then hundredths, then thousandths, and so on, as illustrated below using the number 287.45. Powers of ten are discussed in more detail on page 21 of Chapter 1:

Hundreds	Tens	Units	Tenths	Hundredths
10^2	10^1	10^0	10^{-1}	10^{-2}
2	8	7 ●	4	5

Percentages

A percentage is a fraction with a denominator of 100 and so the expression 25% should be thought of as an abbreviation for $^{25}/_{100}$.

Ratios

These are similar to fractions but are denoted in a slightly different way, and are often used when making comparisons. For example, if when mixing mortar you use 1 bucket of cement for every 4 buckets of sand, the ratio of cement to sand is 1 to 4 and this is written as 1:4. Ratios can be used to compare more than two quantities. For example, if concrete requires 5 buckets of sand and 3 buckets of gravel for every 2 buckets of cement then the ratio of sand to gravel to cement is 5:3:2.

The world in which we live does not comprise only whole numbers and whole quantities and so fractions, decimals, percentages and ratios feature strongly in our everyday experiences. It is therefore important that we understand and are able to use these non-integral numbers for our own personal use but also because they need to be taught to pupils of primary age as illustrated by the following examples:

● Pupils will start to use simple fractions towards the end of KS1 and by the time they leave primary school they should understand terminology such as *numerator, denominator, proper, improper, mixed number* and so on.

● Decimals should start to feature strongly from the middle of KS2, although many pupils will encounter them in the context of money during KS1.

● Pupils should be introduced to simple percentages towards the end of KS2.

● During KS2 pupils should start to solve simple problems involving ratio and proportion.

Vocabulary

Some people would argue that much of the language associated with fractions is rather old-fashioned and so need not necessarily be introduced to pupils in the primary school. Why use *numerator* and *denominator* when 'top number' and 'bottom number' will suffice? Is it really necessary for pupils to know terms such as 'proper' and 'improper'? Being able to identify whether a fraction is greater than or less than one is far more important than knowing the antiquated name for it. However, the National Numeracy Strategy *Mathematical Vocabulary* book suggests that all of this language should be introduced to pupils before they leave primary school.

When working with fractions, it is important to always refer to the whole object or whole quantity – for example, say 'half a pizza' or 'half a metre' rather than just 'half'. However, with young pupils care will need to be taken in the use of the word 'whole' because it sounds the same as 'hole' and so can cause confusion. One way of overcoming this is to avoid using 'whole' as a noun and so try to use it only as an adjective, for example say *Three-quarters of a whole cake* rather than simply *Three-quarters of a whole*.

It is not uncommon for pupils to read a decimal number

such as 3.25 as 'three point twenty-five'. Listen out for these sorts of errors and explain to pupils that the last two digits do not represent twenty-five. By insisting on the correct use of this sort of language you can assist pupils' understanding of place value in the context of decimals and thus help them to appreciate that 25 and 0.25 are two completely different numbers.

Fractions were used by the Ancient Egyptians nearly four thousand years ago. The notation they adopted involved writing all fractions as the sum of fractions with a numerator of 1. So, for example, the fraction $^7/8$ would be written as $^1/2 + ^1/4 + ^1/8$. This system was also used by the Greeks until about the end of the fifth century.

Amazing facts

An alternative notation used by early civilizations was to write all fractions in terms of a standard denominator and powers of that denominator. The Babylonians' use of 60 as a standard denominator spread to Europe where it persisted until the sixteenth century. This notation had a direct influence on the development of our systems of time (for example 1 hour = 60 minutes) and angular measurement (1 degree = 60 minutes). You might like to consider why they chose 60 (think factors – 60 has got a large number of factors and so sixtieths can be used to represent halves, thirds, quarters, fifths, sixths and tenths, as well as other types of fraction). The Romans chose to use 12 as their standard denominator thus resulting in our pre-decimal monetary system in which 1 shilling = 12 pence and our non-metric system for measuring length in which 1 foot = 12 inches.

Using Babylonian notation, the mixed number 1¼ would be expressed as:

and written as	$1 + ^{15}/60$ 1 15'

The Roman equivalent would be:

and written as	$1 + ^3/12$ 1 3'

Eighths cannot be expressed as an exact number of sixtieths or twelfths and so powers of 60 and 12 would have to be used to denote a number such as $3^7/_8$:

$$3^7/_8 = 3 + {}^{52}/_{60} + {}^{30}/_{3600}$$

and was written as 3 52' 30" by the Babylonians:

$$3^7/_8 = 3 + {}^{10}/_{12} + {}^6/_{144}$$

and was written as 3 10' 6" by the Romans.

Don't worry if you are struggling with these calculations – that is the key point; they are very awkward to work with! It was from this extremely cumbersome method for denoting fractions that decimal notation evolved. If, instead of using 60 or 12 as the standard denominator, 10 is used, then the number $3^7/_8$ begins to take on a more familiar form:

$$3^7/_8 = 3 + {}^8/_{10} + {}^7/_{100} + {}^5/_{1000}$$

which could be written as 3 8' 7" 5''' and is not dissimilar to the 3.875 that we use today. In an essay written at the beginning of the seventeenth century, the English mathematician John Napier used the notation 25, 3' 7" 9''' to represent the number 25.379 and it was only a matter of a few years later that decimal notation as we know it started to be used.

Common misconceptions

● Pupils do not always appreciate that when an object is divided into halves or quarters the resulting pieces are equal. You may well hear pupils saying things such as 'I'll have the big half'. Pick up on these misconceptions and use this as an opportunity to stress that halving does not simply mean dividing into two parts; the parts must also be equal.
● It is not uncommon for pupils to think that, for example, 0.12 is greater than 0.5. This problem arises because they read the digits after the decimal point as 12 and 5 and so clearly lack an understanding of place value in the context of decimals. The solution is to ensure that pupils appreciate what each of the digits represents by asking questions such as *How many tenths are there in this number? What does this 5 represent?* and so on. A number line extending from 0 to 1, marked off in tenths and hundredths is an invaluable teaching aid when discussing these issues with pupils.

● Practical apparatus and visual aids are essential when introducing pupils to fractions. Use cakes, pizzas, sheets of paper, lengths of ribbon, or just about anything that can easily be divided into halves and then quarters.

● When introducing pupils to fractions, always stress that the object or quantity under consideration is being divided into *equal* parts. This important point should be reinforced with pupils of all ages whenever they are working with fractions.

● Always refer to the whole object or the whole quantity, otherwise fractions can become a very abstract concept. The phrase *three-quarters* has little meaning to a child but *three-quarters of a cake* is much easier to grasp.

● Use a number line displayed on the wall when introducing decimals. This should extend from zero to at least one and be sufficiently large for you to divide it into tenths and then again into hundredths.

Teaching ideas

Key concepts and techniques

Equivalent fractions

It is possible for two fractions with different denominators to be equivalent to one another. For example the fractions $5/10$, $2/4$ and $1/2$ are all equivalent to one another. To change a fraction into an equivalent fraction simply multiply both the numerator and the denominator by the same amount as illustrated below. Any multiplier can be used as long as the same one is used for both the numerator and the denominator. In the example below, the multipliers of 2 and then 5 have been used to convert $3/4$ into two equivalent fractions:

Subject facts

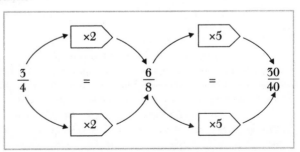

Cancelling or simplifying fractions

This is based on the same principles as those used when creating equivalent fractions above, but this time you divide both the numerator and the denominator by the same amount. So, for example, the fraction $^{30}/_{40}$ can be cancelled down or simplified by dividing both the numerator and the denominator by 10 to give ¾. This can be done in a single stage or in two or more stages. For example, you could divide $^{30}/_{40}$ by 2 to give $^{15}/_{20}$ and then divide by 5 to give ¾.

Comparing and ordering fractions

There are two basic principles to remember when comparing and ordering fractions:

1. If all of the numerators in a set of fractions are the same (for example 1) then you can order the fractions by simply looking at the denominators. The bigger the denominator, the smaller the fraction. So, for example, the fractions $^{1}/_{10}$, $^{1}/_{8}$, $^{1}/_{5}$, $^{1}/_{4}$, $^{1}/_{3}$ and $^{1}/_{2}$ are listed in ascending order based on this principle.
2. If all of the denominators in a set of fractions are the same then you can order the fractions by simply looking at the numerators. The bigger the numerator, the bigger the fraction. So, for example, the fractions $^{1}/_{10}$, $^{2}/_{10}$, $^{3}/_{10}$, $^{5}/_{10}$, $^{6}/_{10}$ and $^{9}/_{10}$ are listed in ascending order based on this principle.

Unfortunately you are not always going to be faced with fractions which have the same numerator or the same denominator and so some additional work is necessary. It is easier to make the denominators the same rather than the numerators and so the first step is to change some or all of the fractions into an equivalent form such that they have the same denominator, called a *common denominator*.
Suppose you want to arrange these three fractions in order, starting with the smallest:

$$^{2}/_{3} \qquad ^{3}/_{4} \qquad ^{5}/_{8}$$

The common denominator must be such that all three denominators can be multiplied by an amount to give the common denominator (see 'Equivalent Fractions' section, page 61). Or put another way, the common denominator must be divisible by each of the three denominators. There are many common denominators for 3, 4 and 8 (for instance 48, 72 and 96), but the lowest common denominator is 24 –

that is, the lowest number which is divisible by 3, 4 and 8. Three fractions must be worked out which are equivalent to $^2/_3$, $^3/_4$ and $^5/_8$, but with a denominator of 24:

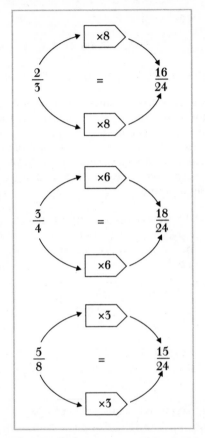

Now that the denominators are all the same it is a relatively straightforward task to arrange the three fractions in order, using the second basic principle identified on page 62.

Another way of comparing and ordering fractions is first to convert them to decimals, using an electronic calculator if appropriate. This conversion is described in a later section (see page 64).

Comparing and ordering decimals and percentages
Comparing and ordering decimals should be fairly straightforward because they are based on a system of place value in the same way that whole numbers are. It is sometimes helpful to write the decimals so that they all have the same number of digits after the decimal point. For

example, if you were ordering these decimals:

| 0.85 | 0.4 | 0.617 |

first write them like this:

| 0.850 | 0.400 | 0.617 |

and then arrange them in order, ignoring the decimal point if you wish.

All percentages are, in effect, fractions with a denominator of 100 and so they can be compared and ordered easily using the basic principles discussed on page 62 – that is, they all have the same denominator (100) and so can be ordered by considering the numerator. In reality you order percentages in the same way that you would order any set of numbers.

Converting from fractions to decimals

A fraction can be converted into a decimal simply by dividing the numerator by the denominator as illustrated by the examples below:

$3/4$ = $3 \div 4$ = 0.75
$5/8$ = $5 \div 8$ = 0.625
$2/3$ = $2 \div 3$ = 0.667 (to 3 decimal places)

Once converted into decimal form it is easy to arrange two or more fractions in order, as discussed in an earlier section.

Converting from decimals to fractions

Make use of your knowledge of place value – that is, what the digits actually represent in terms of the decimal column headings. For example, place value tells us that 0.1 represents $1/10$, 0.2 represents $2/10$, 0.3 represents $3/10$ and so on. Simplify the fraction if possible by cancelling, as in the case of $2/10$ which should be written as $1/5$. Other examples are illustrated below:

0.25 = $25/100$ = $1/4$
0.375 = $375/1000$ = $3/8$ (375 and 1000 are
                            both divisible by 125)
0.45 = $45/100$ = $9/20$ (45 and 100 are
                            both divisible by 5)
0.19 = $19/100$ (cannot be simplified)

Converting between decimals and percentages

The relationship between a decimal and its percentage equivalent becomes obvious if you study a few common examples such as those shown below:

0.25	=	25%
0.75	=	75%
0.15	=	15%
0.10	=	10%

Clearly the digits are the same but the decimal point is in a different position, and so converting from one form to the other is simply a matter of adjusting the decimal point two places in the appropriate direction, using your knowledge of the common examples as a guide. If you don't like learning rules without understanding why they work then think about it carefully for a few minutes; use what you already know and it should all start to make sense. In the first example above 25% means $^{25}/_{100}$ and so place value tells us that this can be written as 0.25.

The percentages that sometimes cause problems are the ones comprising a single digit such as 5%. The decimal equivalent is clearly 0.05 ($^5/_{100}$) rather than 0.5 which is 50%. Fractions of a percent, for example 17½%, also cause problems. In this particular case the decimal equivalent is 0.175 – that is, halfway between 0.17 (for 17%) and 0.18 (for 18%). It should also be obvious that a percentage such as 2½% is 0.025 as a decimal.

Converting from fractions to percentages

If you have understood the conversions explained above, you should be able to convert a fraction into a decimal using division and you should be aware of the relationship between equivalent decimal and percentage forms. Put this together and you have a method for converting a fraction into a percentage. First convert the fraction into a decimal by dividing the numerator by the denominator, and then adjust the decimal point to give a percentage. This is illustrated in the examples below:

$^2/_5$	=	$2 \div 5$	=	0.4	=	40%
$^7/_8$	=	$7 \div 8$	=	0.875	=	87.5% (or 87½%)
$^1/_{16}$	=	$1 \div 16$	=	0.0625	=	6.25% (or 6¼%)

Converting from percentages to fractions

As has been discussed in an earlier section, a percentage is a fraction with a denominator of 100, so all you have to do is write the percentage in this form and simplify if possible by cancelling. This is illustrated in the examples below:

$$55\% = {}^{55}/_{100} = {}^{11}/_{20}$$

$$8\% = {}^{8}/_{100} = {}^{2}/_{25}$$

$$12\tfrac{1}{2}\% = {}^{12\frac{1}{2}}/_{100} = {}^{1}/_{8}$$

Simplifying a ratio

Ratios derived from a real-life situation are often not in their simplest form and so they can be cancelled down in the same way as fractions. For example, if a class comprises 16 boys and 12 girls, the ratio of boys to girls is 16:12. Both of these numbers are divisible by 4 and so the ratio can be simplified to 4:3 – in other words there are four boys for every three girls. The ratios 16:12 and 4:3 are equivalent to one another in the same way that two fractions can be equivalent.

Sometimes a ratio is expressed in such a way that the first number is 1, even if this means that the second number is not an integer. Using the example above, the ratio 16:12 would be simplified by dividing both numbers by 16 to give a ratio of 1:0.75, in other words there are 0.75 girls for every boy. The figures may not be particularly meaningful in concrete terms but they do provide a way of comparing the two quantities and they form the basis of calculations involving ratios and proportions as described in a later section.

Why you need to know these facts

The key concepts and techniques described above form the foundation of all calculations involving fractions, decimals, percentages and ratios. A thorough understanding of these basic principles is therefore essential both in terms of your own ability to calculate and solve problems and also in terms of your teaching, because many of these things need to be taught to pupils during Key Stage 2, as illustrated by the examples below:

● Pupils should begin to understand simple equivalence of fractions, starting with halves and quarters, from the end of KS1 onwards.

● During KS2 pupils should start to develop strategies for

simplifying, comparing and ordering fractions.
● The ordering and comparing of an increasingly more complex range of decimals should feature from the middle of KS2 onwards.
● Pupils should be aware of simple fraction and decimal equivalence in the middle of KS2 and later extend this to include percentages.
● At the upper end of KS2 pupils should encounter situations involving the simplification of ratios and the identification of equivalent ratios.

Vocabulary

In addition to the obvious terminology indicated in the sections above, there are a number of alternative expressions in everyday use which you and your pupils need to be aware of. For example, cancelling fractions is often described in terms of *reducing a fraction to its simplest form* and the word *proportion* is often used to mean 'fraction' as in *What proportion of the class are girls?*.

Common misconceptions

When adding and subtracting fractions, some people find the common denominator by multiplying the denominators of the fractions they are working with. This approach is fine. It will produce a common denominator but it will not always produce the lowest common denominator and so you end up working with unnecessarily large numbers. For example, suppose you were adding $^3/_4$, $^5/_6$ and $^3/_8$. Multiplying the denominators produces a common denominator of 192 when in fact the lowest common denominator is only 24.

Teaching ideas

The concept of equivalent fractions forms the basis of so much of the later work on fractions that it is important to spend a large amount of time practising and reinforcing this work. Use various practical and visual means to reinforce the concepts. For example, you could produce several pictures of the same large bar of chocolate, one divided into halves, another into quarters, another into sixths, another into eighths and so on. Also explore the numerical patterns in the numerators and denominators of sets of equivalent fractions and show how these can be produced by repeated multiplication. For example, the equivalent fractions shown below are produced by repeated doubling:

$$^2/_3 \ = \ ^4/_6 \ = \ ^8/_{12} \ = \ ^{16}/_{24} \ = \ ^{32}/_{48}$$

During Years 5 and 6 pupils should be able to recall instantly an increasing number of conversions between fractions, decimals and percentages. To reinforce this work you could display a large poster-sized table on the classroom wall which summarizes the common conversions. You could also feature these conversions in the mental starter of your lessons (remembering, of course, to remove or hide the poster first!).

Calculations involving fractions, decimals, percentages and ratios

Subject facts

The four rules of fractions

You can only add or subtract fractions if they have the same denominator; in other words you can only add thirds to thirds or subtract quarters from quarters. Fractions therefore often have to be changed to an equivalent form using a common denominator before they can be added or subtracted. An example of this is provided below:

$$\frac{1}{4} \quad + \quad \frac{2}{3}$$

Convert both fractions to twelfths.

$$\frac{1}{4} \quad \overset{\times 3}{\underset{\times 3}{=}} \quad \frac{3}{12} \quad \text{and} \quad \frac{2}{3} \quad \overset{\times 4}{\underset{\times 4}{=}} \quad \frac{8}{12}$$

$$= \quad \frac{3}{12} \quad + \quad \frac{8}{12}$$

$$= \quad \frac{11}{12}$$

When multiplying two fractions you must first ensure that any mixed numbers are changed to improper fractions, for example the mixed number 2½ would need to be changed to $^5/_2$. The next stage is simply to multiply the numerator of the first fraction by the numerator of the second to give the numerator of the answer and to multiply the denominators in a similar fashion. It may well be possible to simplify the answer by cancelling and if the answer is top-heavy it should be changed to a mixed number. An example of this procedure is provided below:

$$2\frac{1}{4} \quad \times \quad 1\frac{2}{3} \quad = \quad \frac{9}{4} \quad \times \quad \frac{5}{3}$$

$$= \quad \frac{45}{12}$$

$$= \quad \frac{15}{4}$$

$$= \quad 3\frac{3}{4}$$

Here the cancelling has been left until after the fractions have been multiplied, although you can cancel before multiplying if you wish – as long as you always cancel a numerator with a denominator. So, for example, it would have been possible to cancel the numerator in $^9/_4$ with the denominator in $^5/_3$, thus producing lower numbers to multiply. Cancelling before doing the multiplication does not affect the final answer.

The division of fractions is based on the principle that dividing by a particular number is equivalent to multiplying by its reciprocal. For example, dividing by 4 is equivalent to multiplying by ¼, and similarly dividing by ½ is equivalent to multiplying by 2 (the reciprocal of 4 is ¼ and the reciprocal of ½ is 2).

The reciprocal of any number is 1 divided by that number. For example, the reciprocal of 5 is 1 divided by 5 which can be written as $^1/_5$.

If the number is a fraction then simply turn it upside down to get the reciprocal. So, for example, the reciprocal of $^3/_4$ is $^4/_3$.

Handy tip

So, in effect, what this means is that you turn the fraction you are dividing by (the divisor) upside down and then multiply. A complete division example is provided below:

$$3\frac{1}{2} \quad \div \quad \frac{3}{4} \quad = \quad \frac{7}{2} \quad \div \quad \frac{3}{4}$$

$$= \quad \frac{7}{2} \quad \times \quad \frac{4}{3}$$

$$= \quad \frac{28}{6}$$

$$= \quad 4\frac{2}{3}$$

As always, it is a good idea to check your answer by looking to see if it looks reasonable. The original question was *How many lots of ¾ can you get from 3½?*. You can get four lots of ¾ from the 3 and so the final answer looks reasonable.

The four rules of decimals
Calculating with decimals should be thought of as a natural extension of calculating with integers. As long as you understand place value in the context of decimals then you can use all of the mental strategies that you are accustomed to using with integers as well as all of the formal and informal pencil and paper techniques you know.

In the case of addition and subtraction, the key is to ensure that you are aware of what each digit actually represents so that you combine the different parts of the numbers in the correct way. For example, when adding two whole numbers you would combine hundreds with hundreds, tens with tens and units with units. You must do the same with decimals otherwise the results are meaningless.

Handy tip

When you are adding or subtracting decimals using pencil and paper methods, write the numbers so that they all have the same number of decimal places. For example, if you are adding 2.875 and 11.5 write the latter as 11.500.

One way of tackling multiplication and division involving decimals is to simply ignore any decimal points, carry out the calculation as if they were integers, and finally decide where the decimal point should go in the answer by estimating roughly what it should be. For example, if you had to work out 1.58×12.3, start by ignoring the decimal points and so work out the answer to 158×123 using whatever method you would normally use. The answer to this is 19434, but you now need to insert a decimal point appropriately to produce the final answer. In the original question the first number is roughly 1.5 and the second is roughly 12 and so the final answer is going to be about 18; in fact we know it should be a bit more than 18 because we have rounded both of the numbers downwards. The final answer must therefore be 19.434.

There should be the same number of decimal places in the answer as in the question. For example, the product of 1.58 and 12.3 (three decimal places in the question) is 19.434 (three decimal places in the answer).

Handy tip

Given that most, if not all, decimal calculations should be carried out in meaningful, real-life contexts it is often possible to dispense with the decimal points altogether by simply converting to different units. So, for example, convert 1.45 metres to centimetres and convert 0.275 kilograms to grams.

Having said all of that, one very important point to remember is that often the process of calculating with decimals is so complex that it is wholly unreasonable to expect anyone to do it using mental or pencil and paper methods. The electronic calculator is therefore the most appropriate tool for the job. In these situations the notion of checking the 'reasonableness' of an answer continues to be the key final stage in the calculating process.

Working out a fraction or a percentage
Sometimes you might need to work out a fraction based on a given situation. For example, if a class comprises 12 boys and 18 girls, what fraction of the class are boys? Here you simply apply your understanding of what a fraction actually is and what the denominator and the numerator represent. There are 30 pupils in the whole class (in other words, the

denominator) and 12 of them are boys (the numerator). The required fraction is therefore $^{12}/_{30}$, which can be simplified to give $^2/_5$.

You might also be asked to work out what percentage of the class are boys. This can be done by simply converting the fraction above into a percentage, using the method described on page 65. It doesn't matter whether you use $^{12}/_{30}$ or $^2/_5$ since they are both equivalent to 40%.

The same approach can be used to convert a test score into a percentage. Suppose a pupil scores 37 out of 40. As a fraction this is $^{37}/_{40}$, which can be converted into a decimal by dividing the numerator by the denominator to give 0.925, and finally presented as 92½%.

Fractional parts

There are many everyday situations in which you need to calculate a fraction of a quantity. For example, when shopping you might pick up a bargain in the sales which is marked as being '$^1/_3$ off' the normal price of £72. But how much are you actually saving? The traditional approach to tackling problems such as this was to turn it into a fractions multiplication with the 72 written as an improper fraction as illustrated below:

$$\frac{1}{3} \times \frac{72}{1} = \frac{24}{1}$$
$$= \text{£24}$$

The trouble with this sort of approach is that it is unnecessarily long-winded and complex. Instead of trying to remember a set of formal rules and notation for dealing with the multiplication of fractions, why not adopt a more 'common sense' approach which is based on an understanding of what fractions are all about? If you want to find one-third of something then it should be obvious that you divide it by three. Similarly, if you want to find five-eighths of something you can divide by 8 to get one-eighth and then multiply by 5 to get five-eighths. Don't be too concerned about setting it out in any formal way using traditional fraction notation as in the above example. Instead, simply divide by 8 and multiply by 5 using whatever calculating strategies you would normally use, including the use of an electronic calculator if more complex numbers are involved.

Percentage parts

The use of percentages to express a proportion of a quantity tends to be more common than the use of fractions. Taxation, interest rates, discounts and pay increases are just a few examples of everyday situations which make use of percentages. Again, the traditional approach relied heavily on the formal procedures and notation for fractions multiplication as illustrated in the example below, where 17½% of £42 is calculated:

$$\frac{17½}{100} \times \frac{42}{1} \quad = \quad \frac{35}{200} \times \frac{42}{1}$$

$$= \quad \frac{7}{40} \times \frac{42}{1}$$

$$= \quad \frac{7}{20} \times \frac{21}{1}$$

$$= \quad \frac{147}{20}$$

$$= \quad £7.35$$

The first step is to write the percentage as a fraction with denominator 100 but the half percent is an inconvenience. This can be eliminated, however, by multiplying both the numerator and denominator by 2 – that is, changing it to an equivalent fraction. The numbers in the resulting calculation can be cancelled (35 and 200 can both be divided by 5 to give $^7/_{40}$ and then the 40 can be cancelled with the 42 to give 20 and 21) before multiplying. This produces a fraction which must finally be converted into pounds and pence.

The procedure described above may well have been the recommended strategy in days gone by but it makes no sense to persist with it today when all that is needed is a basic understanding of percentages and a bit of common sense.

One possible approach is first to find 1% of £42 by dividing by 100 (42p) and then multiply this by 17½ to get the required answer. This calculation can easily be done with an electronic calculator but there is no reason why it cannot be done by a combination of mental and pencil and paper methods.

The working out for another approach is provided below:

$$100\% = £42$$
$$10\% = £4.20$$
$$5\% = £2.10$$
$$2\tfrac{1}{2}\% = £1.05$$
$$17\tfrac{1}{2}\% = £4.20 + £2.10 + £1.05 = £7.35$$

A slight variation is to use the fact that 20% is £8.40 and subtract 2½% from this to find 17½%.

Both of these approaches are based on mental methods and on an understanding of percentages rather than on the ability to remember a formal procedure. Yes, the traditional approach will produce the correct answer, but only as long as you can remember it and execute it correctly.

Percentage increases and decreases
Percentage parts such as those illustrated above are often calculated in the context of a percentage increase or decrease, for example a 5% pay rise or a discount of 10%. One possible way of tackling these sorts of situations is to first work out what the percentage part is and secondly add it to or subtract it from the original value. There is, however, another way of considering percentage increases and decreases.

Suppose you wanted to work out the sale price of a coat which normally costs £65 but has been discounted by 15%. The original price, £65, represents the full price of the coat – that is, 100%. The sale price represents 85% of the original price and so you need to simply work out 85% of £65. This can be done in many different ways but the key point here is that the calculation of 85% is a single-stage process rather than the two-stage process of first calculating 15% and then subtracting the answer from £65.

This single-stage process can be similarly applied to situations involving a percentage increase. Suppose a restaurant bill of £24 was subject to a 12% service charge. The cost of the meal represents 100% and so the final amount paid is 112%. The task is therefore to work out 112% of £24. This could be done in two stages – that is, work out 12% of £24 and then add it on, but doing it in a single stage is a possible alternative which is illustrated opposite:

```
100%  = £24
10%   = £2.40
1%    = £0.24
2%    = £0.48
112%  = £24 + £2.40 + £ 0.48 = £26.88
```

The approach you choose to adopt (two-stage or one-stage) will probably depend on exactly what it is you need to find out. If it is important for you to know the value of the increase or decrease then it is perhaps best to calculate this first. If you only need to know the final amount then a one-stage calculation can be used.

Percentages with a calculator

Sometimes, when calculating with percentages in the ways outlined above, it is wholly appropriate to use an electronic calculator. Most calculators these days have a percentage key which offers a number of shortcuts as illustrated by the following examples.

Example 1: Convert the fraction $^7/_8$ to a percentage:

Without the percentage key

| 7 | ÷ | 8 | × | 1 | 0 | 0 | = |

With the percentage key

| 7 | ÷ | 8 | % |

Example 2: Work out 35% of £9:

Without the percentage key

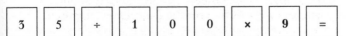

| 3 | 5 | ÷ | 1 | 0 | 0 | × | 9 | = |

With the percentage key

| 9 | × | 3 | 5 | % |

Example 3: Increase £12 by 8%:

Without the percentage key

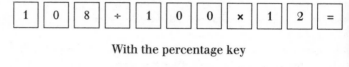

With the percentage key

Example 4: Decrease £65 by 15%:

Without the percentage key

8   5   ÷   1   0   0   ×   6   5   =

With the percentage key

Note: It is important to check to see exactly how your particular calculator operates. The procedures described above work on most calculators, but not necessarily on all of them.

Calculating quantities using ratios

There are many possible situations which make use of ratios but a common one involves working out the quantity of one type of object when you know the quantity of another and the ratio in which they occur. For example, suppose you know that when making jam the ratio of strawberries to sugar is 3:5. How much sugar is needed if you have got 1.5kg of strawberries?

One way of tackling this is to think in terms of equivalent ratios – in other words you must find a value S, representing the weight of sugar, such that the ratio 1.5:S is equivalent to the ratio 3:5. You can create equivalent ratios by multiplication and division in the same way as you can create equivalent fractions. Dividing both numbers in the ratio 3:5 by 2 gives 1.5:2.5 and so the required amount of sugar is 2.5kg.

Another way of solving this problem is to write the ratio 3:5 in an equivalent form but with the first number equal to 1. Dividing both numbers in the ratio by 3 gives the equivalent ratio $1:^5/_3$ or alternatively $1:1^1/_3$ or 1:1.333. This is telling us that there should be $1^1/_3$ kg of sugar for every kilogram of strawberries and so the required quantity of sugar is therefore 1.5 x $1^1/_3$ = 2.5kg.

Suppose you had 4kg of sugar. How many kilograms of strawberries must be mixed with the sugar to produce jam? This time you know the second number in the ratio (the quantity of sugar) and need to work out the first (the quantity of strawberries). You therefore require a ratio equivalent to 3:5, but this time with the second number equal to 1. Dividing both numbers by 5 gives the equivalent ratio $^3/_5$:1 or 0.6:1; in other words there will be 0.6kg of strawberries for every kilogram of sugar. Therefore 4 × 0.6 = 2.4kg of strawberries are needed.

Sharing in a given ratio

Sometimes you may have a quantity which must be shared out in a given ratio. For example, suppose two business partners agree to share their profits in the ratio 3:4. If during a particular month they make a profit of £3500, how much will each partner receive? The ratio 3:4 indicates that there are 7 'shares' to be allocated between the two partners. If £3500 represents 7 shares, then 1 share is £500 and so the first partner (3 shares) will receive £1500 and the second partner (4 shares) will receive £2000.

Calculating with fractions, decimals, percentages and ratios are essential life-skills which you will use both in your personal life and as part of your professional role as a teacher, for example when calculating percentages in an attendance register, or when interpreting the wealth of statistical information circulated to schools by LEAs and the government. You will also have to introduce many of these skills to the pupils you teach depending on their age and ability as indicated by the examples below:

● From the middle of KS2 onwards pupils should be able to find fractional parts of numbers and quantities.
● Towards the end of KS2 pupils should start to find simple percentage parts.
● Mental and pencil and paper calculations involving decimals should feature in the work at the upper end of KS2.
● Pupils should start to solve simple problems involving

Why you need to know these facts

ratios in the middle of KS2 and extend this to include sharing in a given ratio by the time they leave primary school.

Amazing savings

If you placed £100 in a savings account which paid 5% interest per year, how long do you think it would take to double your money? You might be inclined to think that it would take 20 years since 5% of £100 is £5 and $20 \times £5 = £100$. In fact, it would take only 15 years for you to double your money, 33 years for it to grow to £500 and 48 years to grow to £1000. This is because you receive interest on the whole amount of money in your account, not just on the original sum invested. So, for example, during the second year you would receive interest on £105. Situations like this can be modelled easily using a spreadsheet. Enter the starting amount (in this example £100) into cell A1. Then, into cell A2, type the formula:

$$= A1*1.05$$

Use the copy facility to copy this formula down the column into cells A3 to A50. Figures representing the amount of money in the savings account at the end of each year should appear in column A as illustrated below:

	A	B
1	100	
2	105	
3	110.25	
4	115.7625	
5	121.5506	
6	127.6282	

Try using different starting amounts by typing a different number into cell A1. Also try varying the rate of interest by using a slightly different formula. For an interest rate of 10% you would need to type into cell A2 the formula:

$$= A1*1.1$$

and then copy it down the column into the other cells.

Amazing fraction sequences

Here are the first four fractions in a sequence:

$$\frac{1}{2} \quad \frac{1}{4} \quad \frac{1}{8} \quad \frac{1}{16}$$

If this sequence was continued and all of the fractions added together, what do you think the total would be? Try it yourself using the first few fractions in the sequence. You should find that the total is approaching 1. In theory, the total gets closer and closer to 1 without ever getting there, but in practice it does reach 1 because it is not possible to work to an infinite degree of accuracy.

Try it again with this sequence:

$$\frac{1}{3} \quad \frac{1}{9} \quad \frac{1}{27} \quad \frac{1}{81}$$

What would all of the fractions in the sequence add up to this time? You should find that the total approaches ½. If you can't cope with fractions addition then you could always convert them to decimals using a calculator and then work out the sum. Alternatively you could use a spreadsheet to investigate the sums of these sorts of sequences. Into cell A1 enter the fraction one-third by typing the formula:

$$= 1/3$$

Each fraction in the sequence is the previous fraction divided by three, so type the following formula into cell A2:

$$= A1/3$$

Use the copy facility to copy this formula down the column into cells A3 to A20. The first six rows of the resulting spreadsheet should look something like this:

	A	B
1	0.333333	
2	0.111111	
3	0.037037	
4	0.0123456	
5	0.004115	
6	0.001372	

To find the sum of these decimal fractions type the following formula into cell A22:

$$= \text{SUM (A1:A20)}$$

The sum of the sequence (ie 0.5) should be displayed in the cell.

Both of the fractions sequences discussed above are called *infinite sequences* – that is, they can be continued ad infinitum. However, infinite sequences such as these do, in practice, have a definite or finite sum. As has already been demonstrated, the first sequence has a sum of 1 and the second a sum of ½.

Amazing race

Greek mythology tells of a race between the great warrior Achilles and a tortoise. Achilles could run ten times as fast as the tortoise and so he gave the tortoise a 100 metres head start. Now, in the time it took Achilles to run the first 100 metres the tortoise progressed one-tenth of this distance – that is, 10 metres. Achilles then had to make up the 10 metres, but while he was doing this the tortoise progressed a further metre. Then, while Achilles made up the metre the tortoise travelled one-tenth of a metre, and while Achilles made up the one-tenth of a metre the tortoise travelled one hundredth of a metre, and so on. This sequence of events would continue infinitely and so Achilles would never be able to catch up with the tortoise!

The paradox described in this story is not dissimilar to the infinite sequences discussed in the 'Amazing fractions sequences' section above. The total distance in metres that Achilles needed to run in order to catch the tortoise is:

$$100 + 10 + 1 + {}^{1}/_{10} + {}^{1}/_{100} + {}^{1}/_{1000} \dots$$

This is an infinite sequence just like those discussed above, and like the earlier ones it also has a finite sum. Use a spreadsheet to find the sum of this infinite series and therefore find out how far Achilles had to run in order to catch the tortoise.

An amazing will

A farmer died and in his will asked that his 17 horses be shared out as follows:
● half of them to be given to his wife
● one-third of them to be given to his son
● one-ninth of them to be given to his daughter.

The family were completely baffled by this, but their mathematically-minded solicitor was able to sort it out. He owned a horse of his own and so added it to the others to make a total of 18 horses. Now he was able to give half (9) to the farmer's wife, one-third (6) to the son, one-ninth (2) to the daughter, and still have his own horse left over for himself. Can you work out the mathematics behind this amazing tale?

The farmer was either incredibly clever (and also realized that the solicitor would come to the rescue with his own horse), or incredibly poor with fractions. Try adding the three fractions together and see what you find. The answer provides the reason why the instructions in the will were impossible to carry out. (The three fractions $1/2$, $1/3$, $1/9$ do not add up to 1.)

The Golden Ratio

The following set of numbers is called the *Fibonacci Sequence*, named after the 12th century Italian mathematician Leonardo of Pisa who was better known as Fibonacci:

> 1, 1, 2, 3, 5, 8, 13, 21, 34...

The first two numbers are both one and all subsequent numbers are the sum of the previous two numbers. The next number in the sequence above is therefore $21 + 34 = 55$.

The ratios of consecutive numbers in the sequence are as follows:

1:1		
1:2		
2:3	which can be written as	1:1.5
3:5	which can be written as	1:1.667
5:8	which can be written as	1:1.6
8:13	which can be written as	1:1.625
13:21	which can be written as	1:1.615
21:34	which can be written as	1:1.619
34:55	which can be written as	1:1.618

These ratios are getting closer and closer to what is called the Golden Ratio, the value of which is 1.618 to three decimal places. This is a very important number and crops up frequently, but not just in mathematics, for example:
● If you start the Fibonacci Sequence with numbers other

than 1 and 1, the ratios of consecutive terms will still approach the Golden Ratio (although the sequence itself will no longer be the Fibonacci Sequence – this must start with two 1s).

● It is supposed to be an aesthetically pleasing ratio, and so the lengths and widths of many paintings and photographs are in the Golden Ratio.

● It features strongly in the natural world. For example, the ratio of the height of your navel above the ground to your height should be close to the Golden Ratio.

Amazing conversions

Any two consecutive numbers in the Fibonacci Sequence discussed above provide an amazing way of converting miles into kilometres and vice versa. For example, 5 miles is approximately 8 kilometres, and 8 miles is approximately 13 kilometres, 13 miles is approximately 21 kilometres, and so on. Use multiples and combinations of these numbers to convert distances which do not actually appear in the sequence. For example, if you know that 8 miles is 13 kilometres then you can quickly deduce that 24 miles is roughly 39 kilometres.

Common
misconceptions

Combining percentage changes.

Despite being used widely in everyday life, there are a few common misconceptions which surface when people calculate with percentages. The first involves a percentage increase followed by a percentage decrease of the same magnitude. Surely if a shop increases prices by 10% one week and then decreases them by 10% the next, then everything will be as it was a fortnight ago? Well, actually no, it won't. In fact, the customers will be better off than they were a fortnight ago. Suppose a basket of groceries originally cost £10. After the 10% price increase the same basket of groceries will cost £11. Now if you decrease £11 by 10% (£1.10) the groceries will cost only £9.90. It all boils down to the fact that the increase is 10% of £10 and the decrease is 10% of £11.

The other common misconception concerns the order in which percentage increases or decreases are applied. Suppose a department store reduces prices by 10% in the summer sale and then for the last few days of the sale reduces the sale prices by a further 25% (this reduction is 25% of the sale prices, not of the original prices). Another department store does things the other way round. It reduces everything by 25% in the sale and then by a further

10% for the last few days. Which store is offering the best deal? Try it yourself with some actual figures and you'll discover that it makes not a penny difference because the order in which the discounts are applied does not affect the result. The same would be true of two percentage increases applied in a different order. It also applies to fractions. What would you rather have, a half of quarter of a pizza or a quarter of half a pizza? Assuming the pizzas had the same topping and were the same size to start with, it wouldn't matter because the two portions would be identical.

Multiplication makes things bigger.

Many people wrongly believe that multiplication always makes a quantity or a number bigger and division always makes it smaller. Some teachers may even be guilty of telling this to their pupils. These beliefs are correct if you restrict your multipliers and divisors to numbers greater than 1, but if you multiply by a fraction or decimal between 0 and 1 this will have a reducing effect. Similarly, dividing by a fraction or decimal between 0 and 1 will have an enlarging effect. For example, if you divide 2 by 0.5 you are, in effect, finding how many halves there are in 2 and so the answer is of course 4. Similarly, if you work out 2 divided by 0.1 (in other words find how many tenths there are in 2) you get 20. Try it for yourself with a calculator and get your pupils to try it as well.

Misinterpreting ratios.

A common misconception involving the use of ratios is to confuse the ratio of the two quantities under consideration with the ratio of one quantity to the total. For example, if in a class of children the ratio of boys to girls is 2:3 a common error is to think that $^2/_3$ of the class are boys. In reality $^2/_5$ are boys and the remaining $^3/_5$ are girls.

Teaching ideas

Knowing what you do not have to teach with regard to fractions is just as important as knowing what you do, so don't spend valuable time teaching pupils how to carry out complex arithmetic involving the addition, subtraction, multiplication and division of fractions. Instead, ensure that pupils understand the concept of a fraction and are able to use and apply a few basic principles in meaningful, real-life situations.

Similarly, ensure that work on decimals is carried out using appropriate contexts such as money and measurement. Don't make pupils do complex calculations involving decimals just for the sake of it.

When teaching percentages make use of headlines in newspapers, advertisements in magazines and the packaging of everyday items purchased in the supermarket (25% extra free!). Working with real-life resources such as these will motivate pupils much more than figures plucked from a maths textbook.

Resources

● Use a variety of practical apparatus, including commercially available resources such as multilink cubes and pattern blocks when introducing pupils to fractions.
● A large number line displayed across the classroom wall is an invaluable aid when introducing pupils to decimals. Initially this could extend from 0–1 and be marked off in tenths. Later you could divide each of the tenths into hundredths and also extend the line to include decimal numbers beyond 1. Fraction and percentage equivalents, written on small pieces of card, could also be attached to the line.
● Use an electronic calculator to explore the relationship between fractions, decimals and percentages.
● Reinforce the equivalence of fractions, decimals and percentages by making sets of cards or dominoes for matching activities.

The following activities can be found in the Scholastic book *Further Curriculum Bank: Number* Key Stage 1 and focus on the topics covered in this chapter: 'Shade half' on page 34; 'Fractions with pattern blocks' on page 35.

The following activities can be found in the Scholastic book *Further Curriculum Bank: Number* Key Stage 2 and again focus on the topics covered in this chapter: 'Fractions with pattern blocks' on page 18; 'Congruent halves' on page 21; 'Multilink make half' on page 23; 'Estimating decimal multipliers' on page 74; 'Number centipedes' on page 77; 'Double or halve bingo' on page 78.

Chapter 4

ALGEBRA

Can you remember what algebra was all about when you were at school? It probably involved things such as expanding brackets, factorizing algebraic expressions, changing the subject of a formula, substituting numbers in place of letters, solving equations, and so on. These are all important techniques, particularly for anyone who wants to study mathematics at a high level, but to be honest they do not feature strongly in the everyday life of a typical adult. The aim of this chapter is to show that algebra is much more than a set of abstract routines such as those listed above and that there are alternative ways of introducing algebra which are less intimidating than some of those used in the past. This chapter will also show that many aspects of algebra are of direct relevance to the primary curriculum despite the fact that the word 'algebra' has virtually disappeared from the Mathematics National Curriculum Programmes of Study for Key Stages 1 and 2.

Patterns and relationships

Early algebra is all about pattern; being able to identify visual and numerical patterns, continuing a pattern, using the pattern to make predictions, and finally being able to make general statements about patterns and relationships.

Visual patterns

Visual patterns can be seen all around us, particularly
repeating patterns in which shapes, symbols, colours and
various combinations of these extend in a line, repeating in
a fixed way. Examples of repeating patterns can be found in
fabrics and on the wallpaper and borders which we all use
to decorate our homes. Here are some examples which
could be made using cubes or counters or simply drawn on
paper:

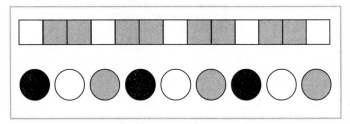

Sets of objects can also be arranged in such a way that they
produce a visual pattern as illustrated by the two examples
below – one using cubes and the other using matchsticks.
These are not repeating patterns but each shape in the
sequence is produced according to a consistent rule,
resulting in a clear visual pattern.

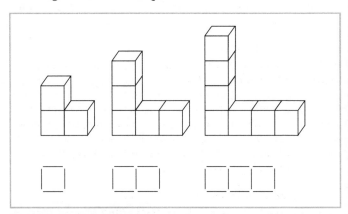

Numerical patterns

Often there is a numerical pattern associated with a visual
pattern. For example, in the arrangements of cubes above,
the numbers of cubes in each 'L' shape are 3, 5 and 7. There
is a clear pattern in this sequence of numbers. Similarly, the
numbers of matchsticks in each of the shapes above are 4, 7
and 10, again following a clear sequence.

Continuing a pattern

Once a visual pattern has been identified it should be possible to continue the pattern by considering it in purely visual or physical terms. It is not essential to consider any numerical patterns that may exist, although the numbers do provide additional clues as to what should come next. For example, once you have identified the numerical pattern in the 'L' shapes (3, 5, 7...) you can extend this sequence to help you construct or draw the next few shapes. Similarly, the pattern in the numbers of matchsticks used in the first three shapes (4, 7, 10...) can be extended to help you to make the fourth, the fifth, the sixth, and so on.

Patterns can often be continued in more than one direction. Suppose the matchstick shapes shown above are in fact the second, third and fourth shapes in a sequence. What then, does the first shape look like? In other words, what comes before the shapes shown above? You could be forgiven for thinking that the required shape comprises no matchsticks at all (because no squares requires no matchsticks) but by examining the numerical sequence closely it becomes apparent that this is not the case. Working backwards, the numbers of matchsticks are 10, then 7, then 4. These numbers are decreasing by three and so the required shape comprises a single match. The key point to remember is that any rule which is used to generate a visual or a numerical pattern must be applied consistently.

Making predictions

Once a pattern has been identified, and perhaps continued further, it should be possible to use your understanding of the pattern to make predictions further down the sequence without actually having to construct, draw or write down all of the intervening items. For example, it should be possible to quickly predict how many cubes will be needed to make the tenth 'L' shape (21) or how many matchsticks to make the twentieth shape (61).

Making generalizations

Once you have identified the pattern, continued the pattern, and predicted particular values further along the sequence, the next stage is to make a general statement which will enable you to quickly predict any value in the sequence.

For example, when predicting the number of cubes in the tenth 'L' shape you can think of this in terms of 3 cubes in the first shape plus 9 lots of 2 (because you add 2 cubes each time to get the next shape in the sequence). Similarly

the twentieth 'L' shape will comprise 3 starting cubes plus
19 lots of 2, and the hundredth 'L' shape will comprise 3
starting cubes plus 99 lots of 2, and so on:

'L' Shape	Cubes
5th	$3 + (4 \times 2)$
10th	$3 + (9 \times 2)$
20th	$3 + (19 \times 2)$
100th	$3 + (99 \times 2)$

Suppose you wanted to predict the number of cubes in the
nth 'L' shape, where n could be any number. You would do
this in exactly the same way as the predictions shown
above; you would subtract 1 from n (because with the 5th
shape you multiply by 4, with the 10th you multiply by 9 and
so with the nth you multiply by $n - 1$), multiply it by 2 and
finally add the answer to 3. This can be written as:

$$3 + (n - 1) \times 2$$

but can be simplified by making use of some of the key
concepts and laws discussed in Chapter 2. The
commutative law tells us that $(n - 1) \times 2$ is the same as
$2 \times (n - 1)$ and by applying the distributive law you can
write it as $2n - 2$ ($2n$ is a shorthand way of writing $2 \times n$).

So the expression:

$$3 + (n - 1) \times 2$$

can be written as:

$$3 + 2n - 2$$

which simplifies further to give:

$$1 + 2n \quad \text{(or } 2n + 1\text{)}$$

So the general statement that can be made about this
sequence is that the nth 'L' shape will have $2n + 1$ cubes. By
substituting values in place of n, you can quickly work out
the number of cubes. Try it yourself using some of the
values discussed above such as 10, 20 and 100.

Identifying relationships

Each of the matchstick shapes shown above has a number of characteristics which can be recorded in numerical terms. For example the number of *squares* can be recorded for each shape, as can the number of *matchsticks*. If we define a *join* as a point where two or more matchsticks meet, then we can record this as well. These three attributes (squares, matchsticks and joins) will vary according to the shape that has been made and so they are often referred to as *variables*. The table below summarizes these variables for the first six shapes in the sequence:

	Squares	Matches	Joins
Shape 1	1	4	4
Shape 2	2	7	6
Shape 3	3	10	8
Shape 4	4	13	10
Shape 5	5	16	12
Shape 6	6	19	14

A relationship exists which links the number of squares to the number of matchsticks. This can be thought of as a rule connecting the two variables which is true for every shape in the sequence. By studying the two columns of numbers carefully, it becomes apparent that to get the number of matchsticks you must treble the number of squares and then add one.

As you read down the columns, one of the variables increases by one while the other increases by three. This gives a clue to the nature of the relationship between the two variables – it will involve multiplication by 3.

Handy tip

This relationship can be expressed simply in words:

> *The number of matchsticks is three times the number of squares plus one.*

It can also be expressed in a more formal way using mathematical symbols:

$$\text{Matchsticks} = (3 \times \text{Squares}) + 1$$

If the letters m and s are used as abbreviations then this becomes:

$$m = (3 \times s) + 1$$

which can be written as:

$$m = 3s + 1$$

This relationship or rule is true for every shape in the sequence. Check it yourself using the numbers in the table. Once the relationship has been established it can be used to work out the number of matchsticks for any given number of squares.

A similar relationship links the number of squares and the number of joins. See if you can work it out for yourself, using the handy tip below if necessary.

Handy tip

As you read down the columns, one of the variables increases by one each time while the other increases by two. The relationship between the two variables will involve multiplication by 2.

The relationship is expressed in a variety of ways below, ranging from the informal to the very formal:

> *The number of joins is double the number of squares plus two*
>
> $$\text{Joins} = (2 \times \text{Squares}) + 2$$
>
> $$j = (2 \times s) + 2$$
>
> $$j = 2s + 2$$

You may well have come up with a very different but still perfectly valid way of expressing the relationship between squares and joins as illustrated below:

> **The number of squares is half the number of joins less one**
>
> Squares = (½ × Joins) − 1
>
> s = (½ × j) − 1
>
> s = ½j − 1

The relationships $j = 2s + 2$ and $s = ½j − 1$ are just two different ways of saying the same thing. One expression implies the other in the same way that $4 + 3 = 7$ implies that $7 − 4 = 3$ and $7 − 3 = 4$. The use of the mathematical symbol for 'implies' is demonstrated below:

$$j = 2s + 2 \Rightarrow s = ½j − 1$$

Why you need to know these facts

Much of what has been discussed above is more relevant to the Key Stage 3 Programme of Study than that at Key Stage 2. However, it is important for primary schools to start to lay the foundations for the formal algebra which will be covered in the secondary phase. Activities involving the identification and continuation of both visual and numerical patterns should therefore be offered to all pupils and many may be capable of moving into 'prediction mode'. Specific examples of what is expected of pupils of different ages is provided below.

• Pupils in Reception should be capable of making simple repeating patterns using practical apparatus.
• From Year 1 onwards pupils should start to work with simple numerical sequences such as those generated by counting on in twos, fives, tens, and so on.
• During Key Stage 2 pupils should develop the ability to recognize and explain patterns and relationships, to continue patterns, to make predictions and to generalize.
• By the end of Key Stage 2 some pupils might be capable of producing an expression for the nth number in a simple sequence.

Algebra

Vocabulary

When considering patterns and relationships don't rush too quickly on to using formal algebraic notation involving letters. Instead, allow pupils to describe and explain patterns and relationships using everyday language until they have fully developed an understanding of the basic concepts.

Amazing facts

The word 'algebra' is derived from a book written by the 9th century Arabian mathematician Al-Khowarizmi, the title of which was *Al-jebr W'almuqabala*. The first part of the title, Al-jebr, means 'transposing a quantity from one side of an expression to another' and the second 'simplifying the resulting expression'. Both of these remain key algebraic techniques today.

Common misconceptions

Many people make the mistake of thinking that the letters used in algebra represent objects and so read $3m$ as 'three matchsticks', $2a$ as 'two apples' and so on. The 'm' in $3m$ represents a number – in other words a quantity of matchsticks – but it is not simply an abbreviation for the word 'matchsticks'. Try to stress this to pupils and avoid telling them that, for example, $2a + 5b$ means '2 apples plus 5 bananas'. This misconception is not helped by the fact that when dealing with measures something such as 12m means 'twelve metres' and so the 'm' is in fact used as an abbreviation.

Teaching ideas

● Allow pupils to explore visual patterns using multilink cubes, counters, matchsticks, and so on. Later, these resources can also be used to look at numerical patterns as has been discussed earlier in this chapter.
● Encourage pupils to describe, explain and discuss the visual and numerical patterns they have generated.
● Use various number grids to explore numerical patterns, for example a 100-square, a multiplication tables square and calendars. Ask pupils to choose any row, any column or any diagonal on these grids, to write down the sequence of numbers, to describe the pattern, and to write down the next few numbers in the sequence.
● *Pascal's triangle*, named after the 17th century French mathematician Blaise Pascal, is an excellent source of number sequences. Here are the first seven rows of the triangle:

```
                1
              1   1
            1   2   1
          1   3   3   1
        1   4   6   4   1
      1   5  10  10   5   1
    1   6  15  20  15   6   1
```

Each number is the sum of the two numbers immediately above it. Ask pupils to fill in additional rows of numbers to get them used to the idea of following a rule consistently. Then ask them to look for special sequences of numbers within the triangle. If you look carefully you should be able to find natural numbers (see page 9 of Chapter 1) and triangular numbers (see page 48 of Chapter 2). Also, work out the sum of each row to produce a doubling sequence.
● When exploring relationships between two variables, tabulate the results on a spreadsheet. This will allow you to quickly plot the values as points on a graph and demonstrate that a relationship does in fact exist.

Formulae, equations and identities

Using a formula

A formula provides a means of expressing a rule or relationship involving two or more variables. You have already seen one or two formulae in the previous section, for example, the one which describes the relationship between the number of matchsticks and the number of squares is:

$$m = 3s + 1$$

Subject facts

Here are a few other examples of formulae that you may be familiar with:

$P = 2L + 2W$	Where P is the perimeter of a rectangle, L is the length of the rectangle and W is the width.
$V = LWH$	Where V is the volume of a cuboid, L is the length of the cuboid, W is the width and H is the height.
$A = \pi R^2$	Where A is the area of a circle, π is pi (3.14) and R is the radius of the circle.
$F = {}^9/_5C + 32$	Where F is a temperature in degrees Fahrenheit and C is a temperature in degrees Celsius.

A formula is used to work out the value of one variable when you know the values of all the others. For example, you can use the first formula above to work out the value of P if you know the values of L and W. So if L is 7cm and W is 5, then:

$$P = 2L + 2W$$
$$= 2 \times 7 + 2 \times 5$$
$$= 24\text{cm}$$

L = 7cm

W = 5cm

The fourth example above can be used to convert temperatures from Celsius to Fahrenheit. Suppose you want to know what 20 degrees Celsius is in Fahrenheit.

$$F = {}^9/_5C + 32$$
$$= {}^9/_5 \times 20 + 32$$
$$= 36 + 32$$
$$= 68°F$$

Creating a formula for a given situation

Sometimes it is beneficial to produce a formula which describes a given situation. For example, suppose an electricity company works out your quarterly bill by charging 12p per unit used plus a fixed charge of £9. The following formula provides a way of working out the quarterly bill for any number of units used:

$$C = 0.12U + 9 \quad \text{Where C is the total cost and U is the number of units used.}$$

So if someone uses 250 units of electricity, then:

$$
\begin{aligned}
C &= 0.12U + 9 \\
&= 0.12 \times 250 + 9 \\
&= 30 + 9 \\
&= \pounds 39
\end{aligned}
$$

Suppose you have a square piece of card which measures 20cm by 20cm. Then cut a small square from each corner to produce a shape which looks something like this:

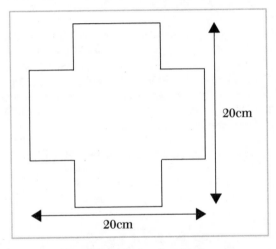

20cm

20cm

If you fold along the dotted lines shown above you can produce an open-topped box. What is the volume of the box? Well obviously it depends on the size of the piece you cut from each corner. Suppose you cut a 4cm by 4cm square from each corner. The resulting box will be 12cm long, 12cm wide and 4cm tall, giving a volume of $12 \times 12 \times 4 = 576$ cm^3. (The units are *cubic* centimetres because the three measurements are being multiplied together.) You could similarly work out the volume for other sizes of cut-outs, but it would be more efficient to produce a formula which describes the situation and therefore be used to work out the volume for *any* size of cut-out.

Let's call the length of the cut-out x (the width of the cut-out is also x because it's a square). The length of the box is therefore 20 minus two lots of x which can be written as $20 - 2x$. The width of the box is also $20 - 2x$. The height of the box corresponds to the size of the cut-out, in other words, the height is x. The volume of the box (length multiplied by width multiplied by height) is therefore given by the formula:

$$V = (20 - 2x) \times (20 - 2x) \times x$$

Where V is the volume of the box and x is the length of the cut-out.

So if the size of the cut-out is 5cm, then:

$$
\begin{aligned}
V &= (20 - 2x) \times (20 - 2x) \times x \\
&= (20 - 10) \times (20 - 10) \times 5 \\
&= 10 \times 10 \times 5 \\
&= 500 \text{cm}^3
\end{aligned}
$$

A formula can also be produced which provides a way of quickly calculating the surface area of the box; that is the area of the card used to make it. The initial piece of card has an area of $20 \times 20 = 400 \text{cm}^2$. From this you cut four small squares, each with an area of x^2 (remember, these cut-outs measure $x$cm by $x$cm). The surface area of the box is therefore given by the formula:

$$A = 400 - 4x^2$$

Where A is the surface area of the box and x is the length of the cut-out.

So if the size of the cut-out is 5cm, then:

$$
\begin{aligned}
A &= 400 - 4x^2 \\
&= 400 - 4 \times 5^2 \\
&= 400 - 100 \\
&= 300 \text{cm}^2
\end{aligned}
$$

Formulae on a spreadsheet

As well as containing text and numbers, cells on a spreadsheet can contain a formula. The formula generally must begin with an equals sign and the variables in the formula are not identified by letters, as in the examples above, but instead by referring to other cells on the spreadsheet. Here is an example of a formula which could be typed into a cell on a spreadsheet:

$$= A1 + A2$$

This formula takes the contents of cell A1 and adds it to the contents of cell A2. The result of the formula will be displayed in the cell into which the formula is typed. So if cell A1 contains the number 7, cell A2 the number 5, and the formula above is typed into cell A3, then A3 will display the result 12.

The formula for working out the surface area of the box discussed earlier could be entered into a cell on a spreadsheet, for example into cell A2. The formula would be:

$$= 400 - 4*A1*A1$$

Note that an asterisk is used to denote multiplication and that squaring has been achieved using repeated multiplication. Values for the size of the cut-out can be typed into cell A1 (which corresponds to the variable x in the formula discussed earlier) and the surface area of the box will be displayed in cell A2.

Equations
These are often derived from a formula such as those considered above. The equation usually contains a single variable, denoted by a letter, which must be calculated using one of several possible methods. For example, in the case of the electricity bill formula, suppose you are told that the total bill is £25.80 and must work out how many units have been used. The formula for working out the bill is:

$$C = 0.12U + 9 \quad \text{Where C is the total cost and U is the number of units used.}$$

If C = £25.80 then this gives:

$$25.8 = 0.12U + 9$$

This statement is an example of an equation. It is true for only one value of U and in order to find this value you must solve the equation.

Similarly, in the case of the surface area of the open-topped box, suppose you know that the surface area is 204cm^2 and are asked to work out the size of the cut-out which will produce this box. The formula for working out the surface area is:

$$A = 400 - 4x^2 \quad \text{Where A is the surface area of the box and x is the length of the cut-out.}$$

So if A = 204cm², then:

$$204 = 400 - 4x^2$$

This is another example of an equation, and to solve it you must find the value of x which makes the statement true.

Solving equations by trial and improvement

One way of solving an equation is to use trial and improvement methods. In other words, have a guess at the answer, see if it works and then adjust your guess accordingly. For example, suppose you are trying to solve the electricity bill equation:

$$25.8 = 0.12U + 9$$

Try U = 100 and you get 21 at the right hand side of the equals sign, which is not enough.
Try U = 150 and you get 27 at the right hand side, which is too much.
Try U = 140 and you get 25.8 which is exactly right.
The solution to the equation is therefore U = 140.

You can use the same approach to solve the surface area equation:

$$204 = 400 - 4x^2$$

Try $x = 5$ and you get 300 at the right hand side, which is too much.
Try $x = 4$ and you get 336, which is even further out and so the guesses are moving in the wrong direction.
Try $x = 6$ and you get 256, which is better.
Try $x = 7$ and you get 204 which is exactly right.
The solution is therefore $x = 7$.

Solving equations using inverses

The electricity bill equation can also be solved by considering inverse operations. The equation is:

$$25.8 = 0.12U + 9$$

This flow diagram illustrates the sequence of operations which are applied to u to produce the answer 25.8:

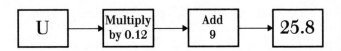

The next flow diagram starts with 25.8 at the right-hand side and works backwards using the inverse of each operation in the original diagram:

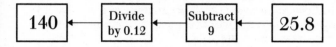

This sequence of inverse operations, applied in the correct order, produces the solution to the equation.

The same approach can be used to solve the equation:

$$3x^2 - 1 = 74$$

The first flow diagram shows what happen to x to produce the answer 74. The second diagram works backwards and applies the inverse operation each time to produce the solution to the equation:

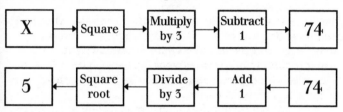

Solving equations using 'Balancing' techniques

An equation can be likened to a set of weighing scales which are in a state of balance. The expression to the left of the equals sign is equal to the expression to the right; the two sides of the equation balance. If you have a set of scales which balance then you can add the same weight to both sides and they will still balance. You can take off the same weight from both sides and they will still balance. You can double, treble or halve the weight on both sides and they will still balance. The same is true of an equation; if you do the same to both sides of the equation then it will remain in balance. This premise can be used to solve equations as illustrated in the two examples below:

$25.8 = 0.12U + 9$	Subtract 9 from both sides
$16.8 = 0.12U$	Divide both sides by 0.12
$140 = U$	
$3x^2 - 1 = 74$	Add 1 to both sides
$3x^2 = 75$	Divide both sides by 3
$x^2 = 25$	Find the square root of both sides
$x = 5$	

This approach is not dissimilar to the one based on flow diagrams since they both make use of inverse operations. In the first example the addition of 9 is removed by subtracting 9 from both sides and the multiplication by 0.12 is removed by dividing both sides by 0.12.

Simultaneous equations

The sum of two numbers is 50 and their difference is 26. What are the two numbers? This could be solved using trial and improvement and requires no knowledge of algebra at all. This approach, however, is sometimes very inefficient and so alternatives based on algebra could be considered. Let's call these two unknown numbers x and y. The information provided can be used to form two equations:

$$x + y = 50$$
$$x - y = 26$$

These are called *simultaneous equations* and to solve them you must find the values of x and y which simultaneously make both statements true. There is nothing wrong with using trial and improvement to solve these, but there is an algebraic alternative which is based on the 'balancing' technique discussed earlier.

Both sides of the first equation are in a state of balance. Both sides of the second equation also balance. So if the left side of the first equation is added to the left side of the second and similarly the right side of the first is added to the right side of the second then the resulting equation will still balance because the same has been added to both sides. This procedure is illustrated below:

$$(x + y) + (x - y) = 50 + 26$$
$$2x = 76$$
$$x = 38$$

If you add y and then subtract y then these cancel out one another.

Now, if $x = 38$ and we already know that $x + y = 50$, then y must be 12. So the solution to the two simultaneous equations is $x = 38$ and $y = 12$.

There is another method for solving simultaneous equations which involves the use of graphs. This is considered later in the chapter.

Identities

When solving an equation, there are a finite number of

solutions (there is usually just one solution). An identity is an expression which looks very similar to an equation, but it has an infinite number of solutions. The unknown variable can take any value and the expression will always be true. Here is an example:

$$7x + 5 = 2x - 1 + 5x + 6$$

Pick any value for x and this expression will always be true. This is because the two sides of the expression are identical. They are simply two different ways of expressing the same thing. $7x$ is identical to $2x + 5x$ and 5 is identical to $-1 + 6$. If an expression is an identity then there is a special symbol which should be used instead of an equals sign, as demonstrated below:

$$7x + 5 \equiv 2x - 1 + 5x + 6$$

Many of the types of formulae discussed in this section crop up in everyday life and so it is important that you are able to understand and use them effectively.

Why you need to know these facts

Formulae may also feature in your professional life, for example, when working out teacher assessment subject levels you may have to use a formula when the levels for each attainment target do not have an equal weighting.

You may also choose to use formulae and equations to find solutions to the problems and investigations you set your pupils. Trial and improvement may well be the appropriate strategy for your pupils to use, but algebra offers you a more efficient alternative.

Formulae and equations also feature strongly in mathematics at Key Stage 3 and so it is important that you are aware of what the next stages will be so that you can lay appropriate foundations.

Some of the mathematics discussed in this section is of direct relevance to the primary curriculum as illustrated by the following examples.

● Even at Key Stage 1, pupils should encounter number sentences with missing numbers that need to be worked out, for example:

$$4 + \boxed{} = 9$$

As pupils progress through the primary school these sorts of problems should gradually increase in complexity and involve a wider range of operations.

Algebra

● From the beginning of Key Stage 2, pupils should be able to tackle problems such as *Find two numbers with a sum of 20 and a difference of 8*. You might like to solve these using simultaneous equations but it is wholly inappropriate for primary pupils to use this approach. Let them stick to trial and improvement.

● At the upper end of Key Stage 2 pupils should start to use simple formulae expressed initially in words and later using letters and symbols. A good example of this is the formula for working out the area of a rectangle.

● By the time they leave primary school some pupils should be capable of writing a simple formula based on a real-life situation and be able to substitute values into a given formula.

Vocabulary

During Key Stage 1 refer to problems such as:

$$7 + \boxed{} = 12$$

as a *number sentence*. During Key Stage 2, introduce the expression *equation* for these sorts of problems.

Amazing facts

You have almost certainly heard one of the many 'think of a number' tricks that have been handed down in the playground from one generation of pupils to the next and possibly even tried to impress your pupils with them! But do you know *why* they work? Algebra can be used to provide an explanation. Here is a typical example:

> Think of a number.
>
> Double it.
>
> Add ten.
>
> Halve the answer.
>
> Take away the number you first thought of.
>
> Your answer is 5!

The other person could think of any number, so let this number be represented by the letter x. Now let's see what happens to x.

Think of a number.	x
Double it.	$2x$
Add ten.	$2x + 10$
Halve the answer.	$x + 5$
Take away the number you first thought of.	5
Your answer is 5!	

Clearly the answer will always be 5 (half of the 10 that was added), regardless of the starting number. You might like to offer this explanation to pupils at the top end of Key Stage 2, perhaps using an appropriate symbol rather than a letter to denote the chosen number. A question mark or a 'thought bubble' (a small cloud) is a good alternative.

Problems with the equals sign.
Many pupils (and teachers) always interpret an equals sign as an instruction to work something out. This belief is reinforced by the use of words such as *makes* instead of *equals* and by the pressing of the equals key on an electronic calculator which results in an answer being worked out. An equals sign is not an instruction at all; it represents equivalence between the expressions either side of it.

The equals sign is often misused both in algebra and when carrying out basic arithmetic as illustrated in the example below:

$$13 \times 24 = 10 \times 24 = 240 + 3 \times 24 = 72 = 312$$

Yes, 13 multiplied by 24 does equal 312 and, if you study the working out carefully, it is possible to make sense of the method. However, what has actually been written down doesn't make sense because each of the expressions between the equals signs are not equal to one another at all. For example, at the beginning 13×24 is not equal to 10×24, and at the end 72 is obviously not equal to 312. These misconceptions can be avoided by writing each line of working out on a new line and keeping the equals signs underneath one another as demonstrated below:

$$
\begin{aligned}
13 \times 24 \quad &= 10 \times 24 + 3 \times 24 \\
&= 240 + 72 \\
&= 312
\end{aligned}
$$

Problems when creating a formula.

Some pupils have problems turning a real-life situation into an algebraic expression. For example, suppose you have a bag containing red counters and blue counters and you are told that there are three times as many red counters as there are blue. A common mistake is to express this relationship as:

$$3r = b$$

when in fact it should be:

$$r = 3b$$
$$\text{or } {}^1\!/_3 r = b$$

The way to avoid this sort of error is to check the formula by using one of the possible combinations of reds and blues. For example, six red, two blue is in line with the original statement and by substituting these in place of r and b it becomes obvious which of the formulae above are valid.

Wrong formula	Correct formula
$3r = b$	$r = 3b$
$3 \times 6 \neq 2$	$6 = 3 \times 2$

How many solutions?

Many people think that if an equation contains only one letter then it has only one solution. This is not always the case. For example, the equation:

$$x^2 - 1 = 15$$

has two solutions; $x = 4$ and $x = -4$. (Remember -4 and $+4$ are both the square root of 16.) Check for yourself by substituting these values in place of x. Most equations which involve squaring the unknown number (these sorts of equations are called *quadratic equations*) have two solutions. Here is another example:

$$x^2 - 4x + 3 = 0$$

which has solutions $x = 1$ and $x = 3$. (They both work and are both solutions.)

However, there are some quadratic equations which have only one solution, for example:

$$x^2 - 4x + 4 = 0$$
$$x = 2$$

and there are some which have no solutions at all, for example:

$$x^2 + x + 1 = 0$$

● From an early age introduce pupils to notation such as

$$7 + \boxed{} = 12$$

to get them accustomed to the idea of an unknown or 'mystery' number.
● Initially use symbols such as question marks, empty boxes and small clouds rather than letters to represent unknown numbers.
● When you do start to use letters in formulae, stress to pupils that the letter represents *any number you want it to* and avoid any suggestion that the letter is an abbreviation for a particular type of object (for example, that $3m$ means 'three matchsticks').
● During oral and mental starter sessions, pose problems such as *I've thought of a number, multiplied it by three, added one and the answer is thirteen. What number did I think of?* As well as developing pupils' mental skills, these sorts of questions encourage them to think about inverse operations. The questions can be adapted to suit various ages and abilities and follow-up activities could involve the use of flow diagrams as described earlier in this chapter.

Functions

A function provides a way of describing the mathematical relationship between two sets of numbers. The best way of illustrating this is in terms of a 'function machine', sometimes referred to as an 'input-output machine'. A number is fed into the machine, subjected to one or more operations, and an output produced. For example, if you were using a 'double it and add one' machine, then an input of 3 would produce an output of 7. Several inputs and outputs for this particular machine are shown in the table below:

Input	Output
1	3
2	5
3	7
4	9
5	11

The table illustrates what happens when specific values are fed into the machine, but it is also possible to state this in general terms. When the number x is fed in, the output is $2x + 1$. We say that the output is a function of x, abbreviated to f(x), and in this particular case

$$f(x) = 2x + 1$$

Sometimes the letter y is used to denote the output and so the function can also be expressed in the following way:

$$y = 2x + 1$$

Both of these expressions can be used to quickly calculate the output for any given input simply by substituting the input value in place of x in the same way as you would substitute values into any formula.

Inverse functions

The inverse of a function 'undoes' the effect of the original function. For example, if a particular function is a 'multiply by three' function, then the corresponding inverse is a 'divide by three' function. The mathematical notation associated with inverse functions is illustrated below:

$$f(x) = 3x$$
$$f^{-1}(x) = {}^1\!/_3 x$$

The letter f is used to denote a function and f^{-1} to denote its inverse.

The inverses of more complex functions, involving two or more operations, can be worked out using flow diagrams like those discussed on page 98 earlier in this chapter. Here is a flow chart for the function $f(x) = 2x + 1$:

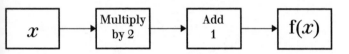

The flow diagram for the inverse function starts at the right-hand side and works backwards using the inverse of each operation in the original diagram:

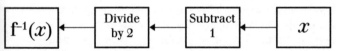

So the inverse function is

$$f^{-1}(x) = {}^1\!/_2(x - 1)$$

You can always check to see if the inverse function is correct by trying a few inputs. For example, if you input 5 into the original function the output is 11. If you now input 11 into the inverse function the output is 5; in other words you are back where you started. The inverse function has 'undone' the effect of the original function.

Co-ordinates

A pair of *co-ordinates* can be used to specify the location of a point on a two-dimensional grid such as the one shown on the next page:

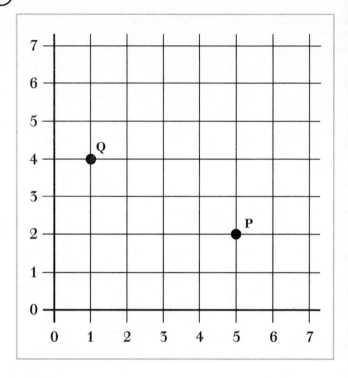

The grid above has two scales; a horizontal scale which is called the *x axis*, and a vertical scale which is called the *y axis*. The position of the point labelled P corresponds to a value of 5 on the *x* axis and 2 on the *y* axis. The co-ordinates of point P are therefore (5, 2).

Point Q has co-ordinates (1, 4). The point where the x axis and the y axis intersect has co-ordinates (0, 0) and is called the *origin*.

Handy tip

A pair of co-ordinates always appear in brackets and are separated by a comma. The *x* co-ordinate is always given first and indicates the horizontal position. The *y* co-ordinate indicates the vertical position.

None of the values on the axes of the grid above are less than zero but by extending the *x* axis to the left and the *y* axis downwards it becomes possible to plot points whose co-ordinates are negative. The resulting grid looks something like this:

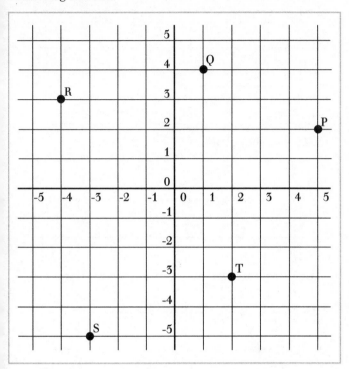

The co-ordinates of the points R, S and T are therefore (–4, 3), (–3, –5) and (2, –3) respectively.

The x and y axes divide the grid into four *quadrants*. Points P and Q are in the first quadrant, point R in the second, point S in the third and point T in the fourth (ie the quadrants are numbered anti-clockwise).

Graphing functions

It has already been stated in an earlier section (see page 106) that a function can be expressed in two different ways, for example:

$$f(x) = 2x + 1$$
$$y = 2x + 1$$

The second notation involves the use of x and y to represent the inputs and outputs and so these could be used as values on the x and y axes of a grid and therefore plotted as co-ordinates. Here are a few possible inputs and outputs for the function above:

x	0	1	2	3	4
y	1	3	5	7	9

These inputs and outputs correspond to the co-ordinates (0, 1), (1, 3), (2, 5), (3, 7) and (4, 9). When plotted on a grid these points all lie on a straight line as illustrated below (only the first four points have been plotted):

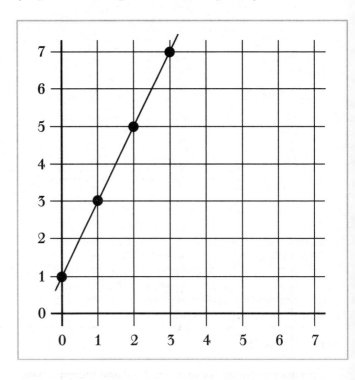

A straight line can be drawn through these points and we say that the *equation* of the line is $y = 2x + 1$. The relationship described by this equation is true for every point which lies on the straight line, in other words the equation is a rule involving x and y which is true for every point on the line.

Not all functions produce a straight line as demonstrated in this example. Here are a few possible inputs and outputs for the function $y = x^2 - 5$.

POCKET GUIDES: NUMBER

x	–3	–2	–1	0	1	2	3
y	4	–1	–4	–5	–4	–1	4

Notice that different values of x (for example –3 and 3) produce the same value of y (9). This is because both '–3 squared' and '3 squared' give the answer 9.

These values correspond to the co-ordinates (–3, 4), (–2, –1) (–1, –4), (0, –5), (1, –4), (2, –1) and (3, 4) which can be joined to produce a curve as shown below:

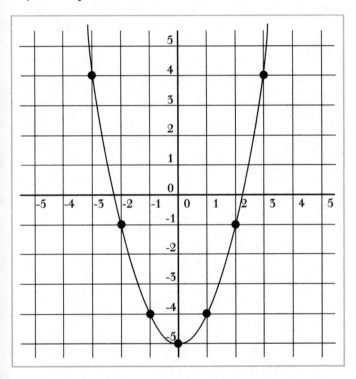

The equation of the curve is $y = x^2 - 5$ and this equation describes the relationship between x and y for every point on the curve.

The equation of a straight line
The equation of a straight line can always be written in the form:

$$y = mx + c$$

where m and c can take any values.

Here are the equations of three straight lines:

$$y = 2x + 1$$
$$y = 2x + 3$$
$$y = 2x - 4$$

Tables showing points which lie on each line are provided below and the three lines are illustrated on the same graph:

$y = 2x + 1$

x	–3	–2	–1	0	1	2	3
y	–5	–3	–1	1	3	5	7

$y = 2x + 3$

x	–3	–2	–1	0	1	2	3
y	–3	–1	1	3	5	7	9

$y = 2x - 4$

x	–3	–2	–1	0	1	2	3
y	–10	–8	–6	–4	–2	0	2

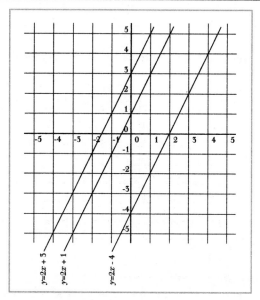

The three equations have something in common; the multiple of x (called the *co-efficient* of x) is 2 in all three cases. The lines themselves also have something in common; they are all parallel.

If two straight lines whose equations are written in the form $y = mx + c$ have the same value of m then they are parallel.

The only thing that is different about the three equations is the number that is added or subtracted. This number is called the *constant* and it corresponds to the point where the line crosses the y axis. This point is called the *intercept*. With the three lines shown above the constants are 3, 1 and –4 and so the lines cross the y axis at (0, 3), (0, 1) and (0, –4) respectively.

If the equation of a straight line is written in the form $y = mx + c$ then the value of c indicates where the line crosses the y axis.

The diagram below shows three more straight lines:

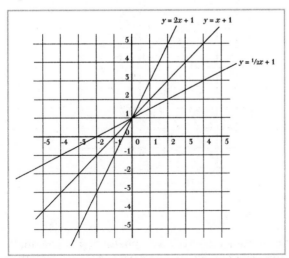

The constant in all three equations is 1 and so the lines all cross the y axis at the point (0, 1). The coefficient of x in each equation is, however, different and consequently the three lines are not parallel. Different coefficients therefore result in lines which slope at different angles. It is noticeable that the steepest line has a coefficient of 2, the next has a coefficient of 1 and the line with the gentlest slope has a coefficient of only ½. The coefficient of x therefore indicates the *gradient* of the line.

Golden rules

If the equation of a straight line is written in the form $y = mx + c$ then the value of m indicates the gradient of the line.

The gradient indicates the rise or fall in a vertical direction for each unit of horizontal change. For example, the line with a gradient of 2 rises 2 squares for each square of horizontal movement. Similarly, the line with a gradient of ½ rises only half a square for each square of horizontal movement.

Not all lines slope upwards from left to right. If a line slopes down then its gradient is negative as illustrated by the three lines below:

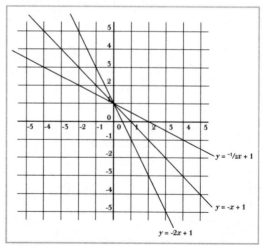

You might not always see the equations of lines such as these presented in this particular form. For example, the line $y = -x + 1$ is often written as $x + y = 1$. These are equivalent ways of stating the same relationship.

Solving simultaneous equations with a graph

Two numbers have a sum of 8 and one number is twice as big as the other. If the letters x and y are used to represent these two numbers then the following equations can be produced from the information given.

$$x + y = 8$$
$$y = 2x$$

Earlier in this chapter it was demonstrated that a pair of simultaneous equations such as this can be solved by trial and improvement and also algebraically. It is also possible to find the solutions by drawing the graphs of the two functions.

The first stage is to identify a set of points that lie on each line. These points are provided in the two tables below:

$x + y = 8$

x	0	1	2	3	4
y	8	7	6	5	4

$y = 2x$

x	0	1	2	3	4
y	0	2	4	6	8

The second stage is to draw the two lines on the same graph as shown below:

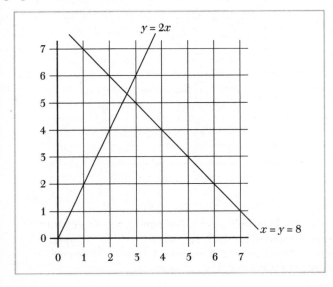

The two lines intersect at the point where $x = 2^2/_3$ and $y = 5^1/_3$ and so these two values provide the solutions to the simultaneous equations and therefore the answer to the original question. Try substituting $x = 2^2/_3$ and $y = 5^1/_3$ into:

$$x + y = 8$$

and

$$y = 2x$$

and you should find that both statements are true; in other words the sum of the two numbers is 8 and one is twice as big as the other.

Why you need to know these facts

Much of the content provided in this section goes beyond what is expected of pupils in the primary school but that does not mean that it is not relevant to primary teachers. In your professional role you are likely to encounter graphs which depict variables plotted as (x, y) co-ordinates, perhaps with an accompanying line or curve from which information has to be read. You may even be expected to produce a graphical representation of data which comprises a pair of variables, for example reading age and chronological age. Sometimes the relationships which exist between these sorts of variables are expressed in the form of an equation which can be used to predict one variable from the other. This makes it vitally important that you understand the basic principles of functions, equations and graphs which have been discussed in this chapter.

Pupils will encounter much of this for themselves during Key Stage 3 but it is important that you start to lay the foundations for this work, particularly in relation to graph work as illustrated by the following examples:
• Midway through Key Stage 2 pupils should start to plot co-ordinates on a grid, but only in the first quadrant.
• This work should be extended during the last year of Key Stage 2 to include co-ordinates in all four quadrants.
• At the same time pupils should also be starting to explore relationships between variables by plotting information on these sorts of graphs. For example, they could plot points which correspond to pairs of numbers with a sum of 12, or plot pairs of numbers whose product is 24, or draw a curve which illustrates the areas of squares of different dimensions, or produce a graph for converting from one currency to another.

With regard to graphs, pupils should be familiar with mathematical language such as *co-ordinates*, *x axis*, *y axis* and *origin* by the end of Key Stage 2. When dealing with co-ordinates in an abstract sense the convention is to use the letters x and y to represent the variables being plotted on the horizontal and vertical axes (lower case letters tend to be the norm and they often appear in italics in printed form). However, when co-ordinates are being used in a real context there is no reason why other, more meaningful letters cannot be used. For example, you might want to produce a graph which illustrates the relationship between a square's length and its area. Here it makes sense to label the horizontal axis l (for length) and the vertical axis a (for area).

The formal language and notation associated with functions, for example f(x) and the equation of a straight line, does not need to be introduced in the primary school.

The full name for co-ordinates is *Cartesian co-ordinates*, named after the 17th century French mathematician René Descartes. He was the first person to make the link between algebra and graph work, resulting in the diagrammatic representation of functions in the ways that have been demonstrated in this chapter.

Points or Squares?
It is common for pupils to think that co-ordinates identify a square on a grid rather than a point. This stems from the common practice of superimposing a grid onto street maps and identifying the squares on the grid using a combination of letters and numbers which resemble a pair of co-ordinates. This is a perfectly acceptable representation, and indeed it is a suitable approach to adopt when introducing co-ordinates to young pupils. However, it is important that the distinction is made between these two slightly different ways of identifying locations on a grid. With the street map approach the letters and numbers are used as labels for the rows and columns of squares and so should appear in the centre of each row or column. Any location, for example B5, refers to a square on the grid, not a specific point. With co-ordinates, however, the numbers on the axes are labels for the grid lines and so should appear adjacent to the lines. When co-ordinates are used to specify location they therefore refer to a single point on the grid.

Vertical and horizontal lines

Don't make the mistake of thinking that diagonal lines are the only lines that have a gradient. What about horizontal lines? Do they slope at all? In other words, do they have a gradient? Well, they certainly don't slope and so the gradient is in fact zero. Does this mean that a horizontal line doesn't have an equation? The general equation of a straight line can be used to answer this question. Remember, any straight line can be written in the form

$$y = mx + c$$

Now if the line is horizontal then the gradient, m, is zero and so the equation becomes:

$$y = c$$

where c is the point where the line cuts the y axis. So the equation of the horizontal line which cuts the y axis at $(0, 3)$ is $y = 3$. Another way of thinking of this is that for every point on this line the y co-ordinate is 3.

At the other extreme are vertical lines which have an infinite gradient. For any particular vertical line the x co-ordinate is constant for any point on the line and so its equation is in the form:

$$x = c$$

For example, the line $x = 5$ is a vertical line which goes through the point $(5, 0)$ as well as through $(5, 1)$, $(5, 2)$, $(5, 3)$, and so on.

Teaching ideas

Encourage older pupils to produce graphs which show relationships between two variables, for example information generated by a mathematical investigation, the results of a science experiment, or everyday situations such as currency conversions. The graph opposite illustrates what a currency conversion line might look like. Suppose the exchange rate for US dollars is such that you get $1.65 for every £1. In order to produce the line you need to work out at least two points which lie on it. You know that for no pounds you will get no dollars and so the line must pass through the origin. You also know, for example, that £100 will buy you 100 × 1.65 = $165. This corresponds to the point (100, 165) on the graph. The conversion line can therefore be produced by drawing a straight line through the points (0, 0) and (100, 165).

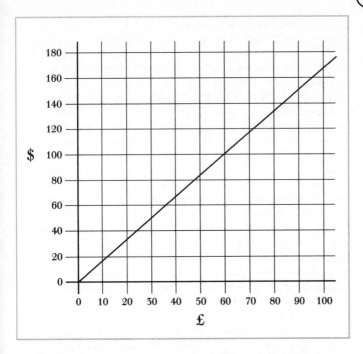

The line can be used to convert from pounds sterling to US dollars and vice versa by simply reading off values which lie on the line. For example, the line shows that £60 is approximately equivalent to $100.

You may also like to tabulate the results of investigations and experiments on a spreadsheet. This allows the data to be plotted as (x, y) co-ordinates on a graph and thus quickly establish the existence of patterns and relationships.

Resources

The Scholastic book *Further Curriculum Bank Activities: Number* Key Stage 1 has a complete chapter which focuses on the topics covered in this chapter. Here you will find eleven activities which provide pupils with an opportunity to explore both visual and numerical patterns and sequences using a variety of practical and worksheet-based materials. Similarly, the Scholastic book *Further Curriculum Bank Activities: Number* Key Stage 2 has a chapter devoted to these sort of activities.

SMILE Mathematics produces a pack of software which focuses on the theme of co-ordinates. Further details can be found at the end of Chapter 2.

If you want to find teaching ideas and resources on the Internet then a good place to start is MathsNet which can be found at *www.anglia.co.uk/education/mathsnet/*. This is a vast site with hundreds of links organized into helpful categories.

If in terms of your own mathematical knowledge and understanding, you would like to find out more about topics such as significant figures then you could visit the BBC Education revision web site at *www.bbc.co.uk/education/ revision*. Follow the link for *GCSE Mathematics* and then select *Number: Intermediate/Higher*. Here you will find links to materials on approximating and estimating and also fractions (which are covered in Chapter 3 of this book). It is also worth exploring other parts of this web site, for example the *Number: Foundation* section has some useful materials covering topics such as negative numbers, ratio and calculating with whole numbers. The *Algebra: Foundation/Intermediate* and *Algebra: Intermediate/Higher* section contain a wide range of materials which could be used in conjunction with this chapter.

Another site worth looking at is the Teacher Training Agency which is responsible for the administration of the QTS Numeracy Skills Test. This site can be found at *www.teach-tta.gov.uk*. Here you will find sample questions, model answers and support materials to help you get to grips with a wide range of mathematical topics.

Appendix

Extract from Annexe D of DfEE Circular Number 4/98

As part of all courses, trainees must demonstrate that they know and understand:	Where you will find this in the book
a. number and algebra i. *the real number system:*	
• the arithmetic of integers, fractions and decimals;	Chapter 2, pages 26–55 Chapter 3, pages 56–84
• forming equalities and inequalities and recognising when equality is preserved;	Chapter 2, pages 32–39 Chapter 4, pages 93–105
• the distinction between a rational number and an irrational number; making sense of simple recurring decimals.	Chapter 1, pages 9–15
ii. *indices:*	
• representing numbers in index form including positive and negative integer exponents;	Chapter 1, pages 20–25 Chapter 2, pages 46–55
• standard form.	Chapter 1, pages 20–25
iii. *number operations and algebra:*	
• using the associative, commutative and distributive laws;	Chapter 2, pages 32–39

• use of cancellation to simplify calculations;	Chapter 2, pages 32–39 Chapter 3, pages 61–84
• using the multiplicative structure of ratio and percentage to solve problems;	Chapter 3, pages 68–84
• finding factors and multiples of numbers and of simple algebraic expressions;	Chapter 2, pages 46–55
• constructing general statements;	Chapter 4, pages 85–120
• manipulating simple algebraic expressions and using formulae;	Chapter 4, pages 85–120
• knowing when numerical expressions and algebraic expressions are equivalent;	Chapter 2, pages 32–39 Chapter 4, pages 93–105
• number sequences, their nth terms and their sums.	Chapter 4, pages 85–93
iv. **equations, functions and graphs:**	
• forming equations and solving linear and simultaneous linear equations, finding exact solutions;	Chapter 4, pages 93–120
• interpreting functions and finding inverses of simple functions;	Chapter 4, pages 106–120
• representing functions graphically and algebraically;	Chapter 4, pages 106–120
• understanding the significance of gradients and intercepts;	Chapter 4, pages 106–120
• interpreting graphs, and using them to solve equations.	Chapter 4, pages 106–120

Number

Glossary

Cardinal number – A number which is used to denote quantity.

Composite number – A number with more than two factors.

Co–ordinates – A pair of numbers (x, y) used to identify the position of a point on a graph.

Counting number – A whole number greater than or equal to zero.

Cube number – A number obtained by 'cubing' an integer: multiplying it by itself and then by itself again.

Cube root – Finding the cube root is the inverse of cubing.

Decimal fraction – Alternative name for 'decimal', in order to distinguish them from vulgar fractions.

Denominator – The bottom number in a vulgar fraction.

Equation – An expression, containing one or more unknowns, which is true for only certain values of those unknowns.

Factor – A positive integer which will divide exactly into the number in question.

Fibonacci sequence – 1, 1, 2, 3, 5, 8, 13, 21. . . Each number is the sum of the previous two.

Formula – An expression which states the relationship between two or more variables.

Function – An expression which states the relationship between two sets of numbers, a set of inputs, and a set of corresponding outputs.

Identity – An expression, containing one or more unknowns, which is true for any values of those unknowns.

Imaginary number – A number which does not exist; it cannot be marked on a number line.

Improper fraction – A vulgar fraction whose numerator is bigger than its denominator.

Index – In the expression 2^5, the index, or 'power', is 3.

Integer – A positive or negative number with no fractional parts.

Inverse – An operation (or sequence of operations) which reverses or 'undoes' the effect of the operation in question.

Irrational number – A number which cannot be expressed as a fraction.

Mixed number – A number comprising whole numbers and fractional parts.

Multiple – The answers in the multiplication tables.

Natural number – A whole number greater than or equal to zero.

Numerator – The top number in a vulgar fraction.

Ordinal number – A number which is used to denote order or position in a sequence.

Origin – The point (0, 0) on a graph.

Percentage – A fraction with a denominator of 100.

Prime number – A number with exactly two factors.

Proper fraction – A vulgar fraction whose denominator is bigger than its numerator.

Quadratic equation – An equation which involves the squaring of the unknown value.

Ratio – A way of denoting proportions or comparing quantities.

Rational number – A number which can be expressed as a fraction.

Real number – A number which can be identified on a number line.

Reciprocal – The reciprocal of a number is 1 divided by that number.

Simultaneous equations – Two equations which contain two unknown values.

Square number – A number obtained by 'squaring' an integer: multiplying it by itself.

Square root – Finding the square root is the inverse of squaring.

Standard form – A way of expressing very large or very small numbers. It comprises a number between 1 and 10 multiplied by a power of ten.

Vulgar fraction – The traditional name for 'fraction', in order to distinguish them from decimal fractions.

Whole number – A positive or negative number with no fractional parts.

x–axis – The horizontal scale on a graph.

y–axis – The vertical scale on a graph.

Number

Index